No matter what it is, the important question always is: "How to do it?"

The mind has many marvelous powers—far more than you have ever dreamed of—and humanity has barely begun the wonderful evolutionary journey that will let us tap into them all at will. We grow in our abilities as we do things.

There are many wonderful things you can do. As you do them, you learn more about the innate qualities of mind and spirit, and as you exercise these inner abilities, they will grow in strength—*as will your vision of your mental and spiritual potential.*

In making a *Love Charm*, or using a *Magic Mirror*, or *Dreaming Lucky Lotto Numbers*, or many other strange and wonderful things, you are extending—just a little bit—the tremendous gift that lies within, the Life Force itself.

We are born that we may grow, and not to use this gift—not to grow in your perception and understanding of it—is to turn away from the gifts of Life, of Love, of Beauty, of Happiness that are the very reason for Creation.

Learning how to do these things is to open psychic windows to New Worlds of Mind & Spirit. Actually doing these things is to enter into New Worlds. Each of these things that we do is a step forward in accepting responsibility for the worlds that you can shape and influence.

Simple, easy to follow, yet so very rewarding. Following these step-by-step instructions can start you upon high adventure. Gain control over the world around you, and step into *New Worlds of Mind & Spirit.*

About the Author

Donald Tyson is a Canadian from Halifax, Nova Scotia. Early in life he was drawn to science by an intense fascination with astronomy, building a telecope by hand when he was eight. He began the university seeking a science degree, but became disillusioned with the aridity and futility of a mechanistic view of the universe and shifted his major to English. After graduating with honors he has pursued a writing career.

Now he devotes his life to the attainment of a complete gnosis of the art of magic in theory and practice. His purpose is to formulate an accessible system of personal training composed of East and West, past and present, that will help the individual discover the reason for one's existence and a way to fulfill it.

To Write to the Author

We cannot guarantee that every letter written to the author can be answered, but all will be forwarded. Both the author and the publisher appreciate hearing from readers, learning of your enjoyment and benefit from this book. Llewellyn publishes a bimonthly news magazine with news and reviews of practical esoteric studies and articles helpful to the student, and some readers' questions and comments may be answered through this magazine's columns if permission to do so is included in the original letter. The author sometimes participates in seminars and workshops, and dates and places are announced in the *Llewellyn New Times*. To write to the author, or to ask a question, write to:

Donald Tyson
c/o The Llewellyn New Times
P.O. Box 64383-831, St. Paul, MN 55164-0383, U.S.A.

Please enclose a self-addressed, stamped envelope for reply, or $1.00 to cover costs.

How To Make and Use a Magic Mirror

PSYCHIC WINDOWS INTO NEW WORLDS

Donald Tyson

1990
Llewellyn Publications
P.O. Box 64383, St. Paul, MN 55164-0383, U.S.A.

International Standard Book Number: 0-87542-831-2
Library of Congress Catalog Number: 90- 33530

First Edition, 1990
First Printing, 1990

Library of Congress Cataloging-in-Publication Data

Tyson, Donald, 1954-
      How to make and use a magic mirror / by Donald Tyson.
        p. cm. –(Llewellyn's how to series)
      Includes bibliographical references.
      ISBN 0-87542-831-2
      Mirrors–Miscellanea. 2. Magic. I. Title. II. Series.
  BF1623.M57T97   1990
  133.4'3--dc20   90-33530
                                            CIP

Cover Design: Christopher Wells

Produced by Llewellyn Publications
Typography and Art property of Chester-Kent, Inc.

Published by
LLEWELLYN PUBLICATIONS
A Division of Chester-Kent, Inc.
P.O. Box 64383
St. Paul, MN 55164-0383, U.S.A.

Printed in the United States of America

OTHER BOOKS IN
LLEWELLYN'S HOW TO SERIES

Other Books by Donald Tyson

The New Magus, Llewellyn, 1988

Rune Magic, Llewellyn, 1989

The Truth About Runes, Llewellyn, 1989

The Truth About Ritual Magic, Llewellyn, 1989

Power of the Runes (kit)

Rune Magic Cards

CONTENTS

INTRODUCTION

This book will show you how to build a true magic mirror that can be used for scrying, astral travel, spirit communication and projecting the will over great distances. It is not a toy or a mere craft project, but a working occult instrument of immense potency. Every step in its construction, from the choice of materials that compose it to the times of its making down to its color and shape, is dedicated to the single function of opening a doorway through the sphere of the Moon to connect the physical and astral worlds.

The black mirror remains mysterious and unknown even within occult circles. It has been passed over in favor of the Tarot, the I Ching, crystals, runes, the Ouija, and a host of other magical tools. Yet it possesses a unique purity of purpose, a nobility in its perfect union of form and function that can scarcely be matched by any other occult device. Its dark, forbidding appearance has earned it a sinister reputation, but the black mirror is not so much evil as chillingly efficient. In stark, no-nonsense simplicity it is like a finely crafted pistol of blued steel and burled walnut, ready for a light, knowing touch to release focused magical power wherever the will directs it.

The shaping of the physical black mirror is only a part of its total making. Equally important is the dedication and lunar charging. To regard only the material that composes the mirror is to value the chrysalis and overlook the butterfly. This is where so many works on mirrors, crystals and other instruments of divination fall short—they devote all their attention to the magical objects themselves, and fail to inform their readers that an instrument of magic is like an iceberg, 10 per cent manifest in the material sensory world and 90 per cent hidden beneath the surface of the unconscious sea. To use another metaphor, the mirror itself is no more than the shadow outline cast by the real mirror, which is a living thing with roots deep in the soil of the unconscious.

Here the vital role of the Moon in all forms of scrying that entail fixation of the sight is clearly and completely explained, perhaps the first time this has been done in so explicit a manner. It is this primary lunar role that necessitates the dedication of the mirror to the Moon and its charging with lunar magnetism. Specific lunar materials compose a natural magnetic fluid condenser used to retain the lunar charge within the glass. Occult symbols, numerical relationships, colors and names of power make up a symbolic fluid condenser that serves a parallel purpose. These lunar fluid condensers allow the mirror to absorb and hold a deep reservoir of occult magnetism in the same way a battery stores electricity.

The mirror functions not in the physical but in the astral world. A complete ritual framework is provided to establish a magical place in the astral. This greatly increases the ease and power with which the mirror may be worked. The ritual also serves to protect the scryer from unwanted interference by spirits, both during the actual scrying and later when the mirror is not in use, by setting a boundary between the astral and everyday worlds that may be selectively opened and closed at will.

Scrying is the most frequent function of the

mirror, but there are many others that are unfamiliar to most practitioners of the art of magic. The mirror acts not just as a window to be looked through, but also as a doorway into strange and distant places both here on Earth and on more subtle planes of being. It is a superior aid to astral travel once the mirror maker has learned to open it, and like any door it may be locked to keep unwanted visitors outside.

Not only can images and, at a higher level of skill, voices be passively perceived through the glass, but magical purpose can also be actively projected using symbolic keys and the agency of spirits. The flow of occult energy through the mirror can be reversed when desired, making it an excellent instrument for communicating with others at a distance or influencing their thoughts and behavior.

The mirror can even act as a suitable receptacle for a discarnate Intelligence which, over time, you have bound to your purposes with ties of affection and comfort. Such a spirit is called a familiar. The way of invoking familiar spirits, and indeed the true nature of spirits in general, is very poorly represented in most occult works because most writers do not know this subject. The method given here for inviting a spirit to reside in the glass is not to be found anywhere else. It is fully integrated with modern occult practices and is based on techniques which the Greek philosophers derived form the Egyptian priests under whom they studied, supplemented by extensive personal research.

Exercises in visualization and breathing, with instructions on proper cleansing, diet, clothing, sitting and environment, prepare the reader to actually use the mirror once it has been assembled. A full account is given of how to scry and what will commonly be seen during scrying sessions. A black mirror worksheet allows each use of the mirror to be recorded accurately in relation to time, place, phase of the Moon, weather, physical and mental state, and other related factors so that over a period of months and years the scryer can plot his or her natural cycles of clairvoyance and astral awareness.

Mindful that some readers may be deterred from attempting to construct the mirror because they lack the necessary craft skills, I have included in Appendix A a much simpler way to make a black mirror. If the instructions are followed accurately, it will possess considerable power. The potency of the mirror comes not from its material but from correct observation of astrological times such as the lunar phases in the construction process, the proper making of the natural and symbolic fluid condensers, the right dedication and charging of the glass prior to use, the employment of an appropriate ritual framework, and most important of all, the magical skill of the user.

Before beginning to build either mirror, the reader should read through the entire book once to gain a complete understanding of the correct sequence of steps in the construction process, and the rationales upon which the directions are based. This will reduce the chance of frustrating errors that waste time and labor.

Anyone can make an effective black mirror if they are willing to devote their time and energy to magically awakening it and giving it life in their unconscious mind. Lack of woodworking experience is no excuse. The nine-sided glass described here is the most powerful black mirror that has ever been designed, yet no matter how beautifully it is crafted, it will only work if the maker has built a part of his or her own soul into it. Dedication without carpentry skill will yield a rough but perfectly serviceable magic mirror. Woodworking skill without dedication will produce only a lifeless object. In the making of the magic mirror it is the heart, not the hands, that matters most.

1

History and Legend

All mirrors are magical. This tends to be forgotten in the modern industrialized world, where mirrors have become so commonplace that they are treated as common objects. Familiarity breeds contempt, and contempt dulls the simple perceptions that are alive in the minds of children and uncivilized peoples.

Who as a child has not stood before a mirror and gazed at the figure reflected within its depths, wondering if there is a flicker of separate awareness in its watchful eyes, wondering a bit fearfully if that awareness is completely friendly? Who has not strained with Alice to see beyond the edges of the glass into the secret places of the mirror world:

> Now, if you'll only attend, Kitty, and not talk so much, I'll tell you all my ideas about Looking-glass House. First, there's the room you can see through the glass—that's just the same as our drawing-room, only the things go the other way. I can see all of it when I get upon a chair—all but the bit just behind the fireplace. Oh! I do so wish I could see *that* bit!...You can just see a little *peep* of the passage in Looking-glass House, if you leave the door of our drawing room wide open: and it's very like our passage as far as you can see, only you know it may be quite

1

> different on beyond. Oh, Kitty! how nice it
> would be if we could only get through into
> Looking-glass House! I'm sure it's got, oh!
> such beautiful things in it!
>
> —Lewis Carroll
> *Through the Looking-Glass*, Chapter One.

Fascination is part of the danger of mirrors. To the savage mind it is a natural thing for the essence of the soul of the person reflected in the glass to become trapped within its mysterious endless depths. This is the myth of Narcissus, who became so enamored with his own reflection in a pool that he pined away with longing and died. In one Orphic myth of Dionysus the god is spellbound when he looks into a mirror and, unable to move, is torn to pieces: "For Dionysus or Bacchus because his image was formed in a mirror, pursued it, and thus became distributed into everything." Olympiodorus, *Commentary on the Phaedo of Plato*, as translated by Thomas Taylor, *The Eleusinian and Bacchis Mysteries*, J. W. Bouton, New York, 1875, Section II, p. 137. Dionysus, it should be noted, is a prophetic god who gave oracles of the future in his temples at Delphi and in Thrace.

James G. Frazer writes:

> The reflection-soul, being external to the man, is exposed to much the same dangers as the shadow-soul. The Zulus will not look into a dark pool because they think there is a beast in it which will take away their reflections so that they die. The Basutos say that crocodiles have the power of thus killing a man by dragging his reflection under water. When one of them dies suddenly and from no apparent cause, his relatives will allege

that a crocodile must have taken his shadow some time when he crossed a stream. In Saddle Island, Melanesia, there is a pool "into which if any one looks he dies; the malignant spirit takes hold upon his life by means of his reflection on the water."

We can now understand why it was a maxim both in ancient India and ancient Greece not to look at one's reflection in water, and why the Greeks regarded it as an omen of death if a man dreamed of seeing himself so reflected. They feared that the water-spirits would drag the person's reflection or soul under water, leaving him soulless to perish. This was probably the origin of the classical story of the beautiful Narcissus, who languished and died through seeing his reflection in the water.

Further, we can now explain the widespread custom of covering up mirrors or turning them to the wall after a death has taken place in the house. It is feared that the soul, projected out of the person in the shape of his reflection in the mirror, may be carried off by the ghost of the departed, which is commonly supposed to linger about the house till the burial....The reason why sick people should not see themselves in a mirror, and why the mirror in a sick-room is therefore covered up, is also plain; in time of sickness, when the soul might take flight so easily, it is particularly dangerous to project it out of the body by means of the reflection in a mirror.

—*The Golden Bough* (abridged edition)
Macmillan, New York, 1951, p. 223.

As a background to his comments on the magical function of ancient Etruscan hand mirrors,

Otto-Wilhelm von Vacano writes in his book:

> Among mankind throughout the world a
> fear of reflections—in water or in shining
> disks—and of their power to cast a spell
> over the soul used to be common; in ancient
> popular customs we find many and various
> precautionary measures designed to shield
> an embryonic life, an unborn or newly born
> child and its mother, from mirrors."
>
> —*Etruscans in the Ancient World*,
> Edward Arnold, London, 1960, p. 9.

This is the seed of living magical belief that lies
at the heart of the seemingly foolish superstition
that to break a mirror brings seven years bad luck,
or the death of a friend or family member.
Variations on this conviction that mirrors have
power to captivate the soul are as old as history:

> One method among the Aztecs of keeping
> away sorcerers was to leave a bowl of water
> with a knife in it behind the door. A sorcerer
> entering would be so alarmed at seeing his
> likeness transfixed by a knife, that he would
> instantly turn and flee.
>
> —Frederick Elworthy, *The Evil Eye*, Ch. Two,
> Collier Books, New York, 1971, p. 83.

In the myth of Perseus, the hero is able to
avoid the petrifying power of the Gorgon Medusa
by only looking at her terrifying face in the mirror-
surface of a polished bronze shield given to him by
the goddess Athene. The reason he is not turned to
stone is that the mirror captures the evil essence of
Medusa and does not allow it to escape, in effect
acting as a magical filter that purges her image of
its essential truth, which is its power.

Jungian analysis tells us that in dreams the symbol of the mirror stands for the objective reality of the dreamer, the naked truth that he cannot bear to face in waking consciousness. This is only another aspect of the magical power of the mirror to catch and hold the essence of things. What you see reflected in a dream may represent the truth stripped bare of the veils of hypocrisy that had been wrapped about it by the unconscious mind. The power of mirrors to reveal hidden truths is alluded to by the apostle Paul when he says: "But we all, with open face beholding as in a glass the glory of the Lord, are changed into the same image from glory to glory, even as by the Spirit of the Lord."(II Corinthians 3:18)

It is hardly surprising that so potent and mysterious an object was used from earliest times for outright magical purposes. But before looking at some examples of the magical mirrors of the past, it is necessary to state that mirrors have not always possessed the flat glass silver-backed form familiar to us today. They have been made in a bewildering variety of shapes and from a wide range of materials.

The earliest mirror was undoubtedly the still surface of water, both natural pools and artificially filled basins. This was also a popular ancient form of magic mirror, the power of which was often associated with a spirit or deity resident at the locality of the pool, or within the stream or spring from which the water used to form the mirror was drawn. The spring that presently flows at the church of Saint Andrew beside the cathedral of Patrai, Greece, was in ancient times in front of a sanctuary of the goddess Demeter. Her priests gave an oracle here that presaged the recovery or death of the sick. They tied a mirror onto a thin cord and balanced it so that its metal surface just kissed the surface of the spring. Then they prayed to Demeter and burned incense in her honor. When the mirror was withdrawn and looked into, it showed the sick person either living or dead (see Pausanias, *Guide to Greece*, B. VII, Ch. 21, Sec. 5).

It was a simple step to draw such magical waters and put them into a vessel where they might be carried about and used at will. E. A. Budge writes : "Magical mirrors were, and are to this day, made of vessels filled with clear water drawn from a well or river;" *Amulets and Talismans*, Ch. XXXVI, Sec. 8, University Books, New York, p. 489.

The ancient Greek practice of "drawing down the Moon" mentioned by Ovid, Lucan, Virgil and others is nowhere clearly described in detail, but seems to have consisted of a ritual in which by chants, dancing, the burning of incense and perhaps sacrifices the reflection of the Moon was magically captured in a vessel filled with water. We can only guess what may have been done with the water afterwards, but it is reasonable to speculate that it was used for curative and divinatory purposes, either on the same night of the ritual or at later times. Indeed, this would seem to be the only logical reason for conducting such a rite.

Thomas and Pavitt in their *Book of Talismans* write:

> In Oudh [in India] a silver basin is filled with water by the people, who hold it so that the orb of the full moon is reflected therein, their doctors recommending this as a remedy for nervous hysteria and palpitation,

patients being directed to look steadfastly
for a while at the reflection, then to shut
their eyes and drink the water at a gulp.
—*The Book of Talismans, Amulets
and Zodiacal Gems,*
Wilshire, Hollywood, 1970, p. 128.

This Hindu practice must be very similar to the
method of the ancient Greeks for capturing the
virtues of the Moon in a magic mirror.

Grillot de Givry describes a multiple magic
mirror called the "three vases of Artephius," the
making and use of which is preserved in two
unpublished manuscripts in the Bibliotheque de L'
Arsenal (mss. No. 3009 and 2344). The device con-
sists of three earthenware vessels on a table with
candles to the right of each vessel. The red vase on
the far left holds oil of myrrh, the green vase in the
middle holds wine, and the white vase on the right
contains water. Alternately the green vase may be
replaced by one of copper and the white vase by
one of glass:

Artephius made an instrument and prepared
it with vases in this manner: by the earthenware vase is the past known, by the copper
vase the present, and by the glass vase the
future. He arranges them in yet another
fashion; that is to say, in place of the earthenware vase a silver vase full of wine is set,
and the copper one is filled with oil, and the
glass with water. Then you will see present
things in the earthen vase, past things in the
copper, and future things in the silver...All
must be shielded from the sun; and the
weather must be very calm, and must have
been so for at least three days. By day you
will work in sunny weather, and by night in

the moonlight and by the light of the stars. The work must be done in a place far from any noise, and all must be in deep silence. The operator is to be garbed all in white, and his head and face covered with a piece of red silken stuff or fine linen, so that nothing may be visible but the eyes...In water the shadow of the thing is seen, in the oil the appearance of the person, and in the wine the very thing itself; and there is the end of this invention.
—*Illustrated Anthology of Sorcery, Magic and Alchemy*, 1929, New York, Causeway Books, 1973, p. 308.

De Givry also describes a traditional method of using a magic mirror to catch a thief. When the detection of a thief was sought, a blessed candle had to be lighted and brought near the mirror, or failing this, near a pot filled with holy water; a virgin had then to pronounce these words: "White angel, holy angel, by thy holiness and by my virginity show me who has stolen this thing!" (Ibid., p. 307) At once the image of the thief would appear in the mirror or upon the water.

A modern variation on this ancient technique of water divination was used in England in the last century, and may still be employed today. The diviner dropped a polished sixpence into the bottom of a glass filled with water and, by staring fixedly at it, perceived the future or things hidden. One may presume that the coin also acted as payment for the divination.

An intimate connection was understood to exist between water and all naturally occurring transparent and translucent materials. Repeating the accepted theory of his day, the Roman naturalist Pliny the Elder says of rock crystal: "for this is hardened by excessively intense freezing. At any rate it is found only in places where the winter snows freeze most thoroughly: and that it is a kind of ice is certain:" *Natural History*, B. XXXVII, Ch. IX, Harvard University Press, Vol. X, p. 181.

Similarly amber, jet, obsidian, glass, diamond and other gems, mica and translucent materials generally were associated, at least implicitly, with water. It is interesting to note in passing that glass, virtually the universal mirror material of modern times, is indeed a liquid rather than a solid, albeit a very, very slow-flowing liquid.

Other liquids were popular for magic mirrors. The ancient Egyptians used a vessel filled with "clear Oasis oil" into which peered a pre-pubescent child, usually a boy, chosen for this purpose because of his purity. While the boy lay on his belly looking into the oil, the magician who was conducting the divination muttered seven times the invocation to the gods (perhaps Thoth, Horus and Isis): "Noble ibis, falcon, hawk, noble and mighty, let me be purified in the manner of the noble ibis, falcon, hawk, noble and mighty." *The Leyden Papyrus*, Dover, New York, 1974, p. 35. The gods then spoke their secrets to the child, who repeated them to the magician.

A variation of this method, which is very old but still employed in modern times (see the description of it in Wilkie Collin's *The Moonstone*), is the anointing of a young boy's palm with oil mixed with lampblack or black ink. Again, it is the child who sees signs in the magic mirror and repeats them to his master:

> Take a new knife with a black handle and make with it a circle in the earth so that you

can sit in it with a boy or a girl less than nine years (old), and anoint the left hand of one (either) of them with olive oil and the black (soot) of a pan, and warn them that they should not look outside the anointed place, and then whisper into his right ear: I adjure you (in the name of) BSKT, K Katriel, MI, Maeniel, that you shall appear unto this child, and you shall give him a proper answer to all that he asks for me, and all this he shall say three times.

—*Babylonian Oil Magic*,
translated by S. Daiches, 1913.
Reprinted in the collection *Three Works of Ancient Jewish Magic*, Chthonios Books,
London, 1986, Part III, pp. 18-9.

There are many variations of the magic mirror in the above-mentioned Hebrew text. For example: "To know whether the child is dead or alive in the bowels of the woman when she is in her severe pains, take a dish full of good oil and she shall see her face in it. If she sees her face, the child is alive, and if not, the child is dead." (Ibid., p. 26)

Another ancient form of a magic mirror was the human thumbnail anointed with oil to make it gleam:

Take a young lad and make a circle in the earth with a knife, the handle of which is black, and prepare the nail of the right thumb until it becomes thin, and take four smooth stones and put (them) in the four rows of the circle, and put the mentioned knife in the middle of the circle and place the lad into it before the pillar of the sun and anoint his nail and his forehead with pure olive-oil, and the lad shall look well at his

nail, and thou shalt whisper into his right
ear this spell: "...I adjure you, princes of the nail,
for the sake (in the name) of the sea and for the
sake of the three lights that are in the universe
[Sun, Moon, Venus], that you should bring the
[demon] king Mimon in this nail, and the queen
shall also come with him."
—*Babylonian Oil Magic*, p. 15.

Almost as old a form of magic mirror is the
shiny blade of a knife, sword or other edged
weapon. In ancient times notable weapons were
given names and thought to possess their own resident spirit, in a sense to be alive. The shedding of
blood over the weapon fed this spirit and kept it
strong. The great German magician Henry
Cornelius Agrippa makes mention of this technique: "they say, if a smooth shining piece of steel
be smeared over with the juice of mugwort, and
made to fume, it will make invocated spirits to be
seen in it." *Three Books of Occult Philosophy*, B. I, Ch.
XLV. Here the juice of the herb, by a process of
magical displacement, has taken the place of blood.

Montague Summers makes mention of Church
prohibitions against scrying into a blade. Peter
Quivil, a 13th-century bishop of Exeter, gave
orders that penitents be forced to confess if they
had recourse to conjurations in a sword or
basin—that is, into magic mirrors of water or polished steel. Summers further relates that in a brief
of February 27, 1318, Pope John XXII ordered the
prosecution of nine witches, who among other
things were accused of making inquiry of and consulting familiar spirits and controls in polished
mirrors. (See *Witchcraft and Black Magic*, Causeway
Books, New York, 1974, p. 78.)

The poet Geoffrey Chaucer also links these

same two kinds of magic mirror:

> But lat us go now to thilke horrible sweryng
> of adjuracioun and conjuracioun as doon
> thise false enchauntours or nigromanciens in
> bacyns ful of water, or in a bright swerd,
> —*Canterbury Tales*
> The Parson's Tale, line 603.

The practice of feeding the magic mirror in its various forms is worldwide: "The Aztecs of Mexico were wont to gaze into small polished pieces of sandstone, and a case is on record where a Cherokee Indian kept a divining crystal wrapped up in buckskin in a cave, occasionally 'feeding' it by rubbing over it the blood of a deer." Lewis Spence, *An Encyclopaedia of Occultism*, 1920, University Books, New York, 1968, p. 127.

Rock crystal has always been, and still is, a popular form of magic mirror. The finest crystal balls are made of natural rock crystal. The English occultist John Dee, counselor to Queen Elizabeth I, used an egg-shaped crystal set in an elaborate wooden frame, and also a black mirror made of obsidian, in his extensive series of spirit communications conducted in the company of his seer, the alchemist Edward Kelly. The results of these remarkable experiments are recorded in *A True and Faithful Relation of What Passed for Many Years Between Dr. John Dee and Some Spirits*, a printing by Meric. Casaubon in 1659 of a portion of Dee's meticulous manuscript record written between 1583-7.

It is to these crystal eggs, or balls, that the poet Edmund Spenser refers when he speaks of the magic mirror of Merlin:

In Dehenbarth, that now South-wales is hight,
What time king Ryence raign'd and dealed right,
The great Magitien Merlin had deviz'd,
By his deepe science and hell-dreaded might,
A looking glasse, right wonderously aguiz'd
Whose vertues through the wyde worlde soone
   were solemniz'd.

It vertue had to shew in perfect sight
Whatever thing was in the world contaynd,
Betwixt the lowest earth and heavens hight,
So that it to the looker appertaynd:
Whatever foe had wrought, or frend had faynd,
Therein discovered was, ne ought mote pas,
Ne ought in secret from the same remaynd;
Forthy it round and hollow shaped was,
Like to the world itselfe, and seemed a world of
   glas.

                                    —*The Faerie Queene*,
                         B. III, Canto II, Stanzas XVIII and XIX.

Although the description is apt to puzzle the
modern reader, Spenser means that the magic mirror was spherical, or at least globular. Elsewhere he
calls it "the glassy globe that Merlin made."
Modern crystal gazers favor a spherical crystal, but
this is a quite recent innovation. As late as the last
century, the crystals were ovoid. De Givry writes of
the English crystal gazers: "They make use by preference of an egg-shaped globe of crystal; Great
Britain does a considerable trade in this article."
Illustrated Anthology of Sorcery, Magic and Alchemy,
p. 307.

Such mirrors need not be large. Gemstones cut
in the form of carbuncles—that is, with a polished
domed surface—could serve this purpose. Pliny
the Elder writes that the Emperor Nero used to

watch the gladiators battling in the arena reflected in the surface of a large polished emerald (*Natural History*, B. XXXVII, Ch. XVI). Emerald, which for the Romans signified a green stone (*smaragdus*), had the fabled medicinal property of strengthening the sight. It is unlikely this particular mirror was magic, but others undoubtedly were. Cornelius Agrippa writes: "And we read that Magnus Pompeius brought a certain glass amongst the spoils from the East, to Rome, in which were seen armies of armed men." *Occult Philosophy*, B. II, Ch. I. It seems likely that Pompey obtained this mirror, or crystal, while pursuing the fleeing armies of Mithradates eastward in 65 B.C.

In old accounts, it is not always easy to know the shape of the mirror or its material. Pliny relates that the Romans sometimes employed black volcanic glass, or obsidian: "This stone is very dark in colour and sometimes translucent, but has a cloudier appearance than glass, so that when it is used for mirrors attached to walls t reflects shadows rather than images." *Natural History*, B. XXXVI, Ch. LXVII, Harvard University Press, Vol. X, p. 155. This, by the way, is very similar to the magic mirror that will be described later in this book.

In his *Amulets and Talismans*, Budge speaks of a set of seven mirrors of metal: "the Kabbalists used seven metal mirrors, each of which bore the name of one of the planets; thus the mirror of the Sun was made of gold, i.e., the solar metal, and could only be consulted with advantage on a Sunday, i.e., the day of the Sun. The mirror of the Moon was made of silver and could only be consulted with advantage on Monday, and so on for the other days of the week. The five other metals were iron

(Tuesday) mercury (Wednesday) tin (Thursday) copper (Friday) lead (Saturday)." *Amulets and Talismans*, pp. 489-90.

The Etruscans used polished bronze disks with elaborately engraved backs. In later Roman times mirrors were made of glass with thin sheets of polished metal spread over their backs. These were generally considered of poor quality because the glass itself was wavy and cloudy. Mirrors were made of silver, which required frequent polishing, and even liquid mercury held behind a glass plate.

Records survive of the magical use of mirrors after the Renaissance, when the mirror began to take on the form we are familiar with today. Catherine de Medici (1519-89) owned such a glass which she reportedly studied to learn the future political happenings in France. This mirror was preserved in the Louvre as late as 1688, but since that time has disappeared. De Givry relates that a Spanish family at Saragossa owned a convex metal mirror "ornamented with a diabolic figure and the words *Muerte, Etam, Teteceme,* and *Zaps.* (Perhaps corruptions of the names of the four spirits who rule the cardinal points.) Figures would appear on the surface of any liquid if the mirror were directed toward it." *Illustrated Anthology of Sorcery, Magic and Alchemy,* p. 307. This last instance sounds like an optical illusion, but this does not mean the mirror was never used for occult purposes.

The use of a magic mirror in the form of a small plate of polished silver is described in the grimoire *The Book of the Sacred Magic of Abramelin the Mage*:

> And you shall continue always your Prayer redoubling your ardour and fervour, and

shall pray the Holy Angel that he may deign to Sign, and write upon a small square plate of silver (which you shall have made for this purpose and which you shall have placed upon the Altar) another Sign if you shall have need of it in order to see him; and everything which you are to do. As soon as the Angel shall have made the Sign by writing, and that he shall have written down some other counsel which may be necessary unto you, he will disappear, but the splendour will remain. The which the Child having observed, and made the sign thereof upon you, you shall command him to bring you quickly the little plate of silver, and that which you find written thereon you shall at once copy, and order the Child to replace it upon the Altar."

—*Sacred Magic of Abramelin*
Dover, New York, p. 82.

Notice the presence of the child to act as a seer, and that the plate is made of silver. The reason the symbol must be copied down quickly is because it is formed in spiderweb-like lines of dew, deposited on the silver by the chill early morning air that enters through the open window. It is specified in the text that the ritual take place in the morning before an open window. As the air warms, the dewy lines would fade and vanish, so haste is essential. The magician is required to perceive an occult symbol in the naturally forming pattern of microscopic droplets which tend to follow the fine scratches that are invariably made when polishing the silver plate.

Perhaps the most famous magic mirror of all plays an important role in the Grimm's fairy tale *Snow White and the Seven Dwarfs*. This mirror was owned by Snow White's wicked stepmother, a sorceress:

> She had a magic looking-glass, and she used to stand before it, and look in it, and say,
>
> *Looking-glass upon the wall,*
> *Who is fairest of us all?*
>
> And the looking-glass would answer,
>
> *You are fairest of them all.*
>
> And she was contented, for she knew that the looking-glass spoke the truth.
> —*Grimm's Complete Fairy Tales,*
> Nelson Doubleday, New York, p. 330.

The significant feature of this glass, which is not clearly described, is its resident Intelligence, not a spirit conjured to appear in the glass, but a familiar bound in a continuing way into the glass itself. Later in this book you will learn a technique for invoking such a spirit and binding it within your magic mirror to act as your aid in using the mirror.

Magic mirrors occur several times in the modern fantasy epic *The Lord of the Rings* by J.R.R. Tolkien. Today Tolkien is best known as a writer of fiction, but his primary work as an Oxford teacher and scholar was philology and mythology. His profound knowledge of ancient languages and legends insured accuracy in the descriptions of occult objects that arise in his tales.

The mirror of the elf queen Galadriel in the forest of Lothlorien is a water mirror of the most ancient type located beside a clear spring in a deep dell open to the sky:

> Down a long flight of steps the Lady went
> into a deep green hollow, through which ran
> murmuring the silver stream that issued
> from the fountain on the hill. At the bottom,
> upon a low pedestal carved like a branching
> tree, stood a basin of silver, wide and
> shallow, and beside it stood a silver ewer.
>
> With water from the stream Galadriel
> filled the basin to the brim, and breathed on
> it, and when the water was still again, she
> spoke. 'Here is the Mirror of Galadriel,' she
> said. 'I have brought you here so that you
> may look in it if you will.'
> —*Lord of the Rings*, Book II, Chapter VII,
> George Allen and Unwin, London, India
> paper edition, 1969, pp. 380-1.

Since the mirror is viewed under the stars, effectively it is a black mirror because it reflects the evening sky. Tolkien, through his character Galadriel, makes the point that the mirror can be directed to reveal specific information on the past, present or future, but will also show secret and hidden things unbidden if approached with a passive, receptive mind. Also, the mirror is not to be trusted as a guide to action:

> Remember that the Mirror shows many
> things, and not all have yet come to pass.
> Some never come to be, unless those that
> behold the visions turn aside from their path
> to prevent them. The Mirror is dangerous as
> a guide of deeds. (Ibid., p. 382)

The other type of mirror described by Tolkien is similar to the glassy globe of Merlin. Tolkien called it a *palantír*, which means in English "far-seer." Originally there were seven *palantíri* occultly linked so that anyone possessing one could communicate over great distances with those who held the others, as well as scry into far times and places. The *palantír* of Minas Ithil is described as "a stone like the Moon," but the one from Orthanc into which the hobbit Peregrin Took scrys is said to be very dark and heavy:

> At first the globe was dark, black as jet, with the moonlight gleaming on its surface. Then there came a faint glow and a stir in the heart of it, and it held his eyes, so that now he could not look away. Soon all the inside seemed on fire; the ball was spinning, or the lights within were revolving.
>
> —*Lord of the Rings*,
> Book III, Chapter XI, p. 615.

These two fictional black mirrors are mentioned here because their symbolism is accurate, and because they demonstrate a common function of magic mirrors that is seldom discussed—the ability to convey over distance the force of a deliberately willed ritual purpose. In both the mirror of Galadriel and the *palantír* of Orthanc the eye of the Dark Lord, Sauron, appears and attempts to project power upon the scryer. The power of Galadriel prevents this intrusion through her water mirror, but through the *palantír* the fallen wizard Saruman is made a thrall to the will of Sauron.

It would not be unfeasible to construct two mirrors, each containing half of a single symbolic identity so that they were really two parts of one mirror, and use these as an aid in telepathic communication. From a technical standpoint, each mirror should be the mirror reflection of the other, as the left hand is a reflection of the right hand. Perhaps it was this type of double mirror that Cornelius Agrippa used in conversing over distance with his occult master the abbot Trithemius, employing the face of the Full Moon as a common link.

It may seem to some out of place when discussing so serious a subject as magic to refer to fairy tales and fantasy epics, but in magic all is not what it seems. Fairy tales and myths are more than mere silly stories, more even than instructive metaphors giving insight into the workings of the mind: they are completely and absolutely true in the strict sense of the word. This is a revelation that usually dawns upon those who are involved in magic for any length of time.

2

The Role of the Moon

The main use for magic mirrors in all their forms has been scrying. The word *scry* is a shortened form of descry: to see or perceive. A scryer is therefore a see-er, or seer, one who discovers hidden or future things at a distance. A second related and by no means unimportant use is communicating with discarnate Intelligences, or spirits. John Dee and Edward Kelly relied mainly upon their crystals and obsidian mirror to hold conversations with a large number of such beings. Occasionally these spirits manifested in physical ways, but usually they appeared to Kelly through the medium of a magic mirror. A third use, little known except to adepts, involves opening a doorway in the mirror through which the soul can travel astrally. A fourth use is the projection of the will upon a magical object of desire using the mirror as an occult channel for the ritually released power. The mirror can be used in a fifth way; to catch and hold a particular spirit to act as a helper in a wide range of magical work.

It is possible to conceive of methods whereby the essence of the soul of a living human being might be captured and held within a mirror, and even destroyed by the shattering of the glass. A person whose soul was imprisoned in this manner would appear to be catatonic, or in a coma.

However, no responsible Magus would attempt such a criminal act, anymore than you would take a gun and shoot someone if you thought you could do it unseen. Such things are very rare, but it is largely through sensational stories about them that the black mirror has gained its evil reputation, which I hope to dispel with this book.

If you look back at the historical and mythical fragments presented in the previous chapter and examine the connecting links, it will at once be clear that all the above powers of the magic mirror stem from and are intimately joined with the powers of the Moon. This seems a sweeping statement, but it is easy enough to demonstrate.

The earliest magic mirror was water. Water is universally recognized as the element of the Moon. In the oceans it reacts with tides to the lunar motions and in the bodies of women, with menstruation. Water is the symbolic element of dreams and the unconscious, both areas of the human psyche that are ruled by the Moon. It is not surprising that water was used in the ancient pagan ritual for drawing down the Moon, so great is this affinity.

The second most ancient magic mirror was rock crystal, which was believed to be a form of petrified ice. Crystal is one of the minerals most closely associated with the Moon. Glass, the material from which virtually all modern mirrors, as well as most crystal balls, are made, is a magical substitute for rock crystal, and as was mentioned before, is in fact a liquid, not a solid.

The best mirror metal, used in both ancient and modern times, is silver. The reason for this is simple—silver reflects 86 per cent of the light that falls on it in the blue range, and 95 per cent in the red range. Compare this with copper, which reflects 48 per cent blue and 90 per cent red; gold, which reflects 29 per cent blue and 92 per cent red; and speculum (an alloy of copper and tin), which reflects 50 per cent blue and 70 per cent red. (Figures are from the Smithsonian Physical Tables.) Even aluminum, used in modern astronomical telescopes because of its resistance to tarnishing, cannot compare with silver as a reflecting medium.

It is the tendency of silver to tarnish black that has made it the recognized lunar metal, more so than the similarity in color between shining silver and the face of the Full Moon. The ancients saw that their silver mirrors periodically blackened but would return to brightness when polished, just as the Moon herself blackens in her phases, but is perpetually renewed. The silver backs of modern mirrors are protected from tarnishing by a layer of paint.

As was mentioned before, Cornelius Agrippa describes the use of shiny steel as a magic mirror when it is prepared by smearing it with the juice of mugwort and heating it until it smokes. The Victorian occultist John Melville in his classic tract *Crystal Gazing and Clairvoyance*, written in 1896, recommends that the crystal gazer eat mugwort during the waxing of the Moon to heighten the clairvoyant powers (*Crystal Gazing*, Weiser, New York, 1970, p. 20).

Why mugwort? Because it is a lunar herb. The Latin name is *artemesia*. Pliny the Elder relates that some authorities believed that the name derived from the goddess Artemis Ilithyia because the plant was used to treat the "troubles of women." (*Natural History*, B. XXV, Ch. XXXVI, Harvard, Vol. VII, p. 189.) The Greek Artemis, who is the same as the Roman Diana, in most classical references is a

Moon goddess. Because of its supposed lunar properties, mugwort was used as an abortive and to hasten the afterbirth. Pliny also says (*Natural. History* B. XXV, Ch. LXXX) that it counteracts the effects of opium (the Moon rules sleep and dreams), and that anyone carrying it cannot be hurt by wild beasts (Diana is mistress of the hunt) or by the Sun (Diana is sister to the Sun). Therefore, mugwort is recommended as an aid to mirror scrying because it attracts and embodies the powers of the Moon and for no other reason.

The Babylonians and Egyptians in their oil divinations used either clear oil of sparkling transparency or oil mixed with lampblack. A silvery brightness and opaque blackness are the two colors of the Moon, both represented in the lunar metal silver. Similarly, the knives of magic have a white and a black hilt (see the *Greater Key of Solomon*, Mathers edition, B. II, Ch. VII). Note that in the Babylonian scrying it is specified that the child who acts as the seer be under nine years. (Nine is the number of the Moon.)

Notice that in the brief issued by Pope John XXII in 1318 he orders the prosecution of nine witches for the crime of conversing with familiar spirits through magic mirrors. It may only be a coincidence, but it is striking that the witches, presumably one group, involved in this lunar activity should number the number of the Moon.

It is of more than passing interest that Spence mentions a Cherokee shaman who kept a divining crystal and fed it with the blood of deer. The stag is the beast of Artemis, and perhaps the most lunar of animals. It is also interesting that divining crystals were egg-shaped. The Moon rules pregnancies and births, and the egg is a potent symbol of new life.

All this serves to explain why English diviners would place a sixpence—a silver coin—into a glass of water. Silver, water, and glass are lunar substances. This is why gypsy fortune tellers are proverbial in their desire to first have their palms crossed with silver. It explains why one form of the oracle of Artephius allows a glass and a silver vessel to replace those of earthenware, and why three vessels in all are used (the Moon has three faces), and why the vessels must be shielded from the Sun (because the Sun is inimical to the operations of the Moon).

Similarly, it is advised that divinations by crystal take place when the Sun is at its lowest point in the sky (Winter Solstice) and that the crystal be kept out of direct sunlight.

By the way, it may seem contradictory that mugwort is said to have power over the Sun, yet the Sun is harmful to the working of the crystal. Both assertions emphasize the adversarial relationship between brother Son and sister Moon. Each limits the force of the other.

It is significant that the magic mirror of Abramelin is made of silver, and that the sign written upon it by the angel is formed with morning dew. Dew was regarded in classical times as a lunar excretion, a type of Moon-sweat, and there were even methods of forcing the Moon to release her dew upon the earth by magically torturing her. When so provoked, it was thought to be poisonous.

Tolkien, whose knowledge of myths and folktales was vast and deep, makes the magic mirror of Galadriel out of water and the *palantír* from crystal. Both mirrors are used at night when the Sun is hidden, the *palantír* under moonlight. Elsewhere another *palantír* is said to be a "stone like the Moon" (*Lord of the Rings*, B. IV, Ch. III, p. 667), and yet a third *palantír*, that of Emyn Beraid, is said to look "towards the Gulf of Lune" and "only to the Sea." (Ibid., Appendix A, p. 1079, note 2). In these fictional details Tolkien reflects the link between magic mirrors and the Moon.

When these many factors are considered together, the evidence is persuasive that the Moon is the single ruling influence on the working of magic mirrors. This does not mean that some tangible force flows from the physical Moon into the physical mirror. It is more useful to say that the occult virtues associated with the Moon manifest their action in the working of magic mirrors in all their varied forms. These lunar virtues govern dreams, visions, illusions, fantasies, physical and mental health, pregnancy and childbirth, mysteries, secrets, things hidden or lost, spirits of the dead, monsters, prodigies, instincts, feelings, the unconscious, and in the body the sexual organs and breasts of women, the intestines and stomach, the blood and other fluids. In these areas and all others associated with the Moon, the magic mirror will prove especially effective because they are in harmony with its essential nature.

By understanding the occult qualities of the Moon we can gain insights that will facilitate the use of the mirror. In almost all cultures the Moon is looked upon as feminine, a goddess who is sister or wife of the Sun. The Sun gives light; the Moon receives and reflects it, in the process changing its color, cooling it, periodically veiling all or part of her face from the eyes of mankind on Earth.

The lunar goddess has many names. As sister of the Sun (Phoebus) she was called Phoebe. The

Romans called her Luna, the Greeks, Selene. Selene is a beautiful goddess with long wings and a golden diadem, full and rounded of face, of middle height, clothed in a long robe and a veil that forms an arch over her head. Above the veil is a crescent. She rides across the night sky in a chariot drawn by two white horses.

In later classical times when the Greek god Apollo became identified with the Sun, it was natural that his sister, the goddess Artemis, became equally identified with the Moon. Artemis is a huntress who bears a bow and quiver. Like her brother she is capable of sending arrows of plague and sudden death among mankind, but also has the power to cure sickness and avert evils. She is especially the protector of the young. The Romans called her Diana. She is a virgin goddess, very modest. She transformed Actaeon into a stag when he saw her nakedness while she was bathing.

Like Athene, another Greek virgin goddess, Artemis is never overcome by the passion of love. The story that she cast a deep sleep over the beautiful youth Endymion in order to be able to kiss him and lie beside his sleeping body is more in character with Selene. It is from the goddess Artemis that the Moon takes some of its more forbidding and baneful qualities.

Another goddess whom the ancients identified with the Moon is Hecate, who is darker by far than Artemis. Originally Hecate was a Thracian divinity, one of the Titans, who was said to rule in heaven, on Earth and in the sea. She became associated with the Mysteries celebrated in Samothrace and Aegina, and is represented as taking part in the search for Persephone after she was carried off by Hades, remaining with Persephone in the

Underworld. This caused her to be looked upon as a goddess of the dead who sent ghosts and demons from the Lower World to haunt the living. She taught sorcery and witchcraft, dwelt at crossroads, in tombs, and was drawn to the blood of murdered men. Dead souls attended her coming, which was warned by the whining and howling of dogs. Not surprisingly, she was consulted for oracles.

Hecate was thought to be threefold in this late period and bore such epithets as *Triformis* and *Triceps*. In heaven she is the same as Selene, on Earth she is Artemis, and in the Underworld she is Persephone. She was described as having three heads, that of a horse, a lion and a dog, symbolizing, respectively, these three goddesses. Since the Moon shows three faces in turn, the full orb (round face of Selene), the waxing and waning crescents (silver bow of Artemis), and the black disk which is hidden (shadowed features of Persephone), there is a natural correspondence between the Moon and Hecate, who is the preeminent goddess of the occult virtues of the Moon.

The position of the Moon in the heavens is also highly significant. Its revolutions define the first of the nine heavenly orbs, or spheres, which the ancients believed surrounded the Earth like nesting crystal shells. God is in the highest heaven. Between the Moon and God are the five visible planets, the Sun, and the fixed stars of the zodiac. The holy angels dwell above the circle of the Moon. God transmits his purposes to the stars. The stars by the agency of their ruling angels in turn send potency to the planets. The planets, by their patterned movements, affect life here on the Earth. But every heavenly virtue first must pass through the sphere of the Moon to reach and affect the Earth. The Moon acts as a kind of gatekeeper, regulating the influence of the heavens upon the Earth, and also the attempts by those on Earth to reach or communicate with the spirits of the heavens.

It will at once be appreciated why the magic mirror, which is a completely lunar device, is so effective in opening the doorway to the worlds of the dead, the spirits and higher angels. Or for those who are uncomfortable in speaking about spirits, why the mirror more than any other tool of magic can provide an easy path to the secret realms of the unconscious. Those who have not experienced close communication with a discarnate Intelligence cannot be convinced there are such things as spirits, but everyone today believes in the "gods" Freud and Jung. The magic mirror can be used as a psychological tool to unlock the mysteries of dreams, obsessions, repressions and compulsions, providing a personal and immediate access to the deepest corridors of the mansion of the mind.

All of the complex and extensive mythological and magical associations of the Moon can be used to aid the working of the magic mirror. By experiencing these lunar symbols mentally and through the physical senses, the user of the mirror is able to attract and heighten the operative virtues of the Moon. This not only makes it easier to get results from the mirror but renders its working more powerful. Modern magical theory does not maintain that there is any special power in the manifest symbols themselves; rather, the symbols produce a harmonic resonance in the deepest well of the psyche of those who fully and openly experience them. The result is increased clairvoyance and a greater ease in communicating with both the depths of the unconscious and with spirit entities, particularly through the medium of the magic mirror, itself a potent lunar symbol.

The accompanying table shows the more effective lunar keys, all of which can be used to lend increased efficacy to the mirror. Some are purely mental, such as the goddesses to be visualized and perhaps represented in drawings or sculpture; others are material objects or living things. All are activated simply by experiencing them in an extended and intense way. This may be done through meditation, visualization and personal contact.

It is more useful to become intimately familiar with just a few lunar symbols so that you know them completely and feel an affinity with them, rather than to surround yourself with dozens of objects, scents and images that you have not taken the time to fully appreciate. For example, prior to scrying in the mirror you might put on a rock crystal pendant previously charged with moonlight, or a silver circlet, along with a woven belt of silver threads, then invoke the aid of the lunar goddess Artemis in a prayer of nine verses—the lunar number. White and black candles might be lighted, representing the lunar colors. In magic it is not how many symbols you use, but how well you know and can experience those symbols.

The writer John Melville, referred to in the previous chapter, says: "remember the strick injunctions of the ancient occultists to utilize the Crystal only during the increase of the Moon," (*Crystal Gazing*, p. 14). The general consensus among modern scryers is that the magic mirror should be used during the waxing phase of the Moon or when the Moon is full. The rationale is that during these phases the powers of the Moon, which preside over magic mirrors and clairvoyance, are stronger. I would support this principle, but would add that some works, such as those involving dreams, nightmares, deeply repressed memories or desires, and communications with the dead, may be done with profit during the dark phase of the Moon. Also, works of evil (though I do not recommend these) are effectively done during the waning and dark of the Moon.

Lunar Correspondences

Land Beasts mouse, stag, white mare, black dog, chameleon, civet, otter, goat, pig, wolf, white tiger, black panther, cat, bull, baboon, bat

Sea Beasts crayfish, cuttlefish, octopus, tortoise, sea turtle, crab, oyster, frog, seal

Birds crow, raven, owl, ibis, ostrich, goose, duck, didapper, heron, gull

Insects flies, beetles, spiders, wasps

Trees willow, olive, palm, silver dogwood

Herbs mugwort, hyssop, rosemary, agnus castus, white rose, peony, camomile

Stones moonstone, rock crystal, jet, obsidian, jade, pearl, black onyx, cat's eye, silver marcasite, ivory, beryl

Metal silver

Colors black, white, silver, purple

Numbers 3, 9, 13, 28, 81, 369, 3321

Elements Water; Earth

Zodiac Sign Cancer

Music violin, flute, harp, recorder, harpsichord, glass organ, cello, wind chimes

Symbols cup, mirror, veil, net, boat, cave, window, keyhole, bed, rope, knots, shadow, pool, eyeglasses, scarf, tie, belt, hook, sickle, house, door, book

Angels Gabriel, Levanael

Spirits Hasmodai, Lunael, Lunaiah

Goddesses Selene, or Luna; Artemis, or Diana; Persephone, or Proserpina; Demeter, or Ceres; Hecate; Isis; Ishtar; Astarte; Hel

Forms round, oval, egg-shaped, crescent, concave, convex

Textures slippery, sleek, flexible, cool, filmy, moist, chitinous, braided, beaded

Tastes salt; insipid, such as the white of an egg

Foods milk, white bread, cream of wheat, arrowroot, white of egg, tapioca, caviar, barley, soda crackers, fish, poultry, rabbit, yogurt, rice; in general, anything tending to blandness, or very salty, anything from the sea, all white flesh and pale dairy products

| Clothing | black or white cotton, purple silk, metallic or silver cloth, silver and crystal jewelry, long flowing garments with loose sleeves and legs, wide hats, veils, long gloves |

3

Fluid Condensers

In his excellent *Initiation Into Hermetics*, the German magician Franz Bardon divides magic mirrors into two kinds: optical mirrors, which include flat mirrors of silver or other polished metals, glass mirrors with silver or black enamel backs, concave mirrors both silver and black, crystals, and the surface of water; and fluid condenser mirrors. (See *Initiation Into Hermetics*, Dieter Ruggeberg, West Germany, 1971, p. 207.)

The notion of a fluid condenser comes from the 18th-century occult theory of animal magnetism, popularized by the Austrian Franz Antoine Mesmer, who proposed in his *De Planetarum Influxu* (1766) that the planets exerted an influence upon the Earth through a universal magnetic fluid. This idea was not really new, but Mesmer was the first to express it in the style of modern science. Later he decided it was possible to concentrate this magnetic fluid for healing effects using metal magnets, and later still, that magnets were unnecessary because the magnetic fluid could be manipulated by the human will, and was in fact a natural part of the human body.

Although a French government commission appointed in 1784 to investigate animal magnetism concluded that there was no such thing, the idea has survived more or less unchanged in occult circles down to the present day because it has proved a useful way of looking at certain observable occult phenomena. It was never disputed that something very strange was happening in Mesmer's treatment clinic, but the commission that denied the existence of animal magnetism made no real attempt to explain the mechanism of the occurrences.

Magnetic fluid is indistinguishable from the ancient Oriental power of *chi* and indeed from the "Force" of the modern *Star Wars* films. It is the *mana* of the Polynesians, the *vril* of the 19th-century fantasy writer Bulwer Lytton, and the Odic force of Baron von Reichenbach.

The Moon is thought to be especially rich in magnetic fluid. This is said to be accumulated upon the surface of the mirror by the magnetic power of the gaze of the scryer, magnetic fluid flowing from the eyes to the mirror. In a sense, this human magnetism primes the pump and polarizes (for want of a better word) the mirror so that it will attract the universal magnetism, particularly that flowing from the Moon, with which the mirror is in natural harmony.

Any physical substance that would increase the accumulation of magnetic fluid upon the surface of the mirror and retain the magnetism there when the mirror is between uses would, of course, be very desirable. Such substances are called *fluid condensers*. These are not necessarily fluids, and may in fact be solids, liquids or vapors, but are called fluid condensers because they condense the magnetic fluid of the Moon. Fluid condensers may be simple, for example, silver or the juice of mugwort, or they may be compound. Bardon gives the recipe for a "universal" fluid condenser that is composed of 15 different herbs (*Initiation Into Hermetics*, p. 118).

The mirror you will be shown how to make is a combination of the optical and fluid condenser types. It utilizes both a natural fluid condenser made up of material substances and a symbolic fluid condenser made up of names of power and visual symbols. A black mirror was chosen as its manifest form because this is an unusual and strikingly beautiful object, completely magical in its function.

Natural Fluid Condenser

The natural fluid condenser is composed of a number of natural materials that have been powdered and mixed together in roughly equal proportions. Each of the ingredients has its own potent and unique association with the Moon. It is not strictly necessary to use all of the things listed, but to insure a balanced working of the condenser at least half a dozen of the ingredients, or reasonable substitutes for them, should be combined. Very little powder is needed, scarcely more than a pinch. It is sprinkled evenly over the back surface of the mirror glass onto a bonding medium that locks it into the body of the mirror.

The following readily obtainable materials make a superior fluid condenser:

> 1 part: fine silver filings
> 1 part: powdered rock crystal
> (or amethyst or beryl)
> 1 part: powdered salt
> 1 part: powdered dried willow
> leaves (or agnus castus)
> 1 part: powdered dried peony

leaves (or white rose)
1 part: powdered dried toadstool
1 part: powdered dried moss
1 part: powdered oyster shell
(or clam shell)
1 part: finely cut cat hair

It is desirable that you use nine ingredients because nine is the strongest number of the Moon. If you cannot get one or more of the above, the following materials may be substituted:

1 part: powdered white eggshell
1 part: powdered fishbone (or scales)
1 part: fine filings of staghorn
1 part: finely cut crow feather
(or seabird or waterfowl feather)
1 part: powdered crab shell
(or lobster shell)
1 part: fine filings of cow bone
1 part: spiderweb
1 part: powdered wasp nest
1 part: powdered silver dogwood leaves

If you are really ambitious, you may combine 13 of the things listed, resulting in a condenser of 13 parts. Thirteen is also a natural number of the Moon because there are 13 lunar months in each year. It is perfectly permissible for you to make up your own list of ingredients, provided you are sure of the occult properties of the materials you select.

Powdered pearl may be substituted for oyster shell. It need not be of the finest quality since it is only going to get pulverized anyway. This is also true of the rock crystal. Pick a small, flawed one, but one that is clear. Also any type of tree that grows in or near marshy earth will serve in place of the willow, but it must be water-loving.

Use a hammer on steel to powder the harder substances; a mortar and pestle is best for grinding up the leaves and other growing things. After you have reduced each material to fine dust, divide them all into equal piles and mix them thoroughly together, then store them away in an envelope or other container where they will not be lost or contaminated with foreign matter.

It is a lot of work to prepare this fluid condenser. Resist the temptation to leave out some of the things simply because they are a little harder to locate. All the ingredients have been selected because they are more or less easy to obtain, in addition to their lunar associations. If you fudge your way through this preparation, you will know in your heart that your mirror is never going to be as perfect or as powerful as you might have made it, and this is a poor way to begin any project.

It is best if you do the final mixing of the nine, or 13, substances on the night of the Full Moon, when the Moon is at its high point in the sky. Failing this, at least be sure the Moon is in the waxing phase. Monday is the best day to combine everything, and if the Full Moon happens to fall on a Monday night, this is best of all.

Symbolic Fluid Condenser

The symbolic fluid condenser operates in the realm of high, or ceremonial, magic on the level of spirits and elemental forces. It creates a sympathetic resonance with the virtues of the Moon in the mind by abstract associations, just as the natural condenser creates a resonance by natural associations, aided by sensory stimuli.

There are certain shapes, numbers and letters associated with the lunar powers, as well as specific recognized spirits with their own names and signs of identification. When these are brought together in a harmonious way, they attract the lunar virtues into the mirror and hold them there.

Procure a sheet of good quality paper that will stand up to the erasure of pencil marks and will hold ink without blotting. Parchment paper, sold by most stationery stores in single sheets for calligraphy work, is excellent. You will need fine-line markers or colored pencils in black, purple and blue.

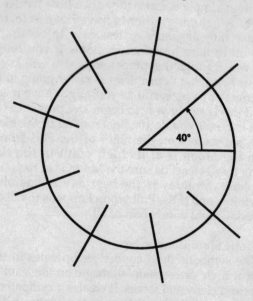

Illustration 1

Alternately, if you are artistic and have a steady hand, you can use black, purple and blue inks or paints and a fine brush. You will also need a set of mathematical drawing instruments—a protractor, a drawing compass, triangles and a ruler. The sets sold for school use work well enough and cost only a few dollars.

Draw a circle of exactly nine inches in diameter with your compass, using a light pencil line. With your ruler, mark the radius of this circle by drawing a line from the center point to the circumference. Using this as a reference, divide the circumference of the circle into nine equal arcs of 40 degrees each with your protractor as shown in illustration 1.

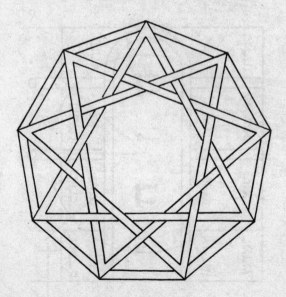

Illustration 2

Now pencil in lightly three equilateral triangles with your ruler, drawing straight lines between the points to make a nonagram. Connect with straight line segments all the points around the circle to form a nonagon which surrounds the three triangles. Double all the lines to the inside so that the lines are 1/4" in thickness. Trace over the lines with your black marker or pen so that the triangles form an interlocking pattern, then when the ink has dried, erase any construction pencil lines that show and color in the nonagram and nonagon with your purple marker, colored pencil or purple ink.

In the open space in the center of the nonagram draw, in black the following symbol:

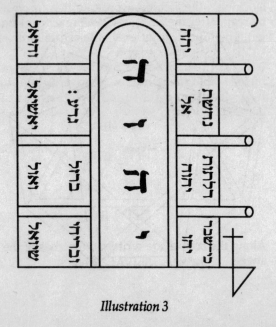

Illustration 3

This is the First Pentacle of the Moon as given in the medieval grimoire *The Greater Key of Solomon*, which is the most authoritative, and perhaps the most ancient, of the grimoires. According to the anonymous writer of the *Greater Key*, this pentacle serves "to call forth and invoke the Spirits of the Moon; and it further serveth to open doors, in whatever way they may be fastened." (*Greater Key of Solomon*, S. L. MacGregor Mathers edition, The de Laurence Company, Chicago, 1914, p. 79). This double function, the calling of spirits and the opening of doors, psychic as well as physical, makes the pentacle perfect for the work of the magic mirror.

If the pentacle is turned a quarter turn counter-clockwise, the Hebrew words written upon it may be read, after the manner of Hebrew, from right to left. The four large letters in the central arch are:

יהוה

which is Tetragrammaton, the most powerful, unspeakable name of God. Above these four letters, also from right to left, are the four divine names of power:

יהו IHV

יהוה IHVH

אל AL

יהה IHH.

Along the bottom are written the names of the four angels שיואל. ShIVAL, Schioel;

VAVL, Vaol; וֹאול

IAShIAL, Yasheil; יאשיאל

and והיאל VHIAL, Vehiel. The remaining two lines of writing are taken from the Hebrew of Psalms 107:16:

כי־שבר דלתות נחשת
ובריחי ברזל גדע :

KI-ShBR DLThVTh NChShTh; VBRIChI BRZL GDAa, which translates: "For he hath broken the gates of brass, and cut the bars of iron in sunder."

Mathers points out that the shape of the pentacle, which is completely different from all the other pentacles of the Moon, and indeed different from all the planetary pentacles in the *Greater Key*, is a rough "hieroglyphic representation of a door or gate." (*Greater Key*, p. 79) The design reminds me of an ancient lock, such as might be used on houses in Roman times. Both associations are appropriate to the function of the pentacle.

Find the center of the back of the symbolic fluid condenser (the hole made by your compass point), and draw with your compass a circle seven inches in diameter, and inside it, another of six inches. Within the smaller circle draw a large traditional seal of the Moon. Below it, between the circles, mark the crescent of the waxing Moon as it would be seen from the perspective of the center of the circles, and after it counterclockwise write the name of the angel of the Moon, Gabriel, GBRIAL:

גבריאל

in Hebrew letters left to right, again so the name

may be read from the point of view of the center of the circles. At 120 degrees, or one-third of the way around, place the symbol of Cancer, the zodiac sign of the Moon, and after it write the name of the archangel of Cancer, Muriel, MVRIAL: מוריאל

At 240 degrees, or two-thirds of the way around, place the symbol of Water, and write the name of the angel of Water, Taliahad, TLIHD: טליהד

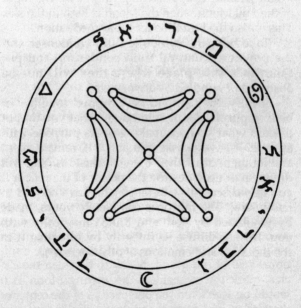

Using colored pencils, markers or paint, color the symbol of the Moon purple, the symbol of Cancer blue-purple, and the symbol of Water blue.

The lines of the circles may also be colored purple, or the space between them lightly filled with purple, but leave the Hebrew letters and the seal of the Moon black, and take care that they remain clearly visible.

After you have cut out this symbolic fluid condenser around the edge of the nonagon it is a good idea to meditate upon its meanings, and upon the qualities of the Moon in general. It is best to do the actual drawing of the symbols during the waxing Moon when it is approaching full, or on the night of the Full Moon when the Moon is high in the sky. This is also the best time for lunar meditation.

Take both the symbolic fluid condenser and the powdered natural fluid condenser, and put them in a safe place where they will not be observed or handled by anyone else.

Ideally, they should be wrapped together in blue or purple silk. It is important that you do not discuss what you are making or its purpose with anyone. If anyone asks you about it, remain silent and let them draw their own conclusions. You will diminish or even destroy the power of the mirror if you idly discuss it with those who have no part in its making. The mirror is completely yours, made by you, used by you, and linked magically with you. Do not diffuse its integrity by mingling it in the thoughts and emotions of other persons.

4

Making the Mirror

The Glass

Before attempting to make the mirror, read thoroughly all the instructions below. This will reduce the chance of costly errors. In fact, it is a good idea to read the whole book once before you try to make anything. You will better understand what you are making and exactly why you are making it.

The mirror is formed from a piece of plate glass cut in the shape of a nonagon. Plate glass is thicker than ordinary sheet glass and usually of better quality. It is flatter and contains fewer defects. Good quality silvered mirrors are made of plate glass; the cheaper ones are of sheet glass. The name "plate glass" comes from its method of manufacture. The hot glass is poured out on flat metal plates, then later polished. "Sheet glass" is rolled out in large sheets or curtains, which results in a waviness that is apparent when it is viewed from an angle.

You can have a glass and mirror shop cut the glass for you, or do it yourself. In either case it is necessary to make a template out of cardboard that is the size and shape of the glass. To make the template, draw a 9 1/2" diameter circle on cardboard or heavy paper, then use your protractor to divide its circumference into arcs of 40 degrees, just as

47

you did when making the symbolic fluid condenser. With a straightedge, connect the points of intersection. Carefully cut out the resulting nine-sided geometric figure. This is your template, which you will trace around to transfer its shape onto the surface of the glass:

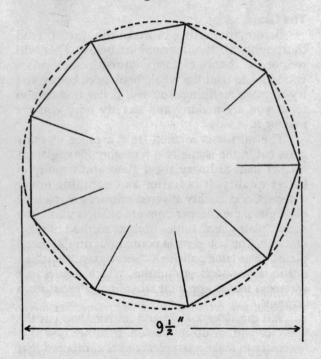

$9\frac{1}{2}$"

The easiest thing to do is just take the template into a glass and mirror shop, where you will likely be buying the glass anyway, and get the service person there to cut the glass using your template as a guide.

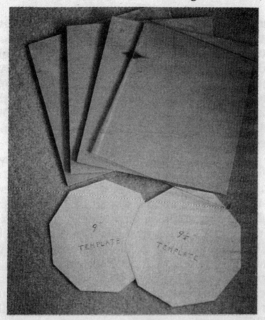

Basic raw materials for the mirror, consisting of three 12-inch squares of 1/4 inch plywood and one 12-inch square of 1/4 inch plate glass. The two templates are made of heavy paper. The smaller one on the left is used to cut out the nine-sided hole in the upper layer of plywood that will form the face of the frame. The larger template is used in cutting the glass.

If you go in and ask for a nonagon in plate glass that will fit inside a 9 1/2" circle, you will probably only get a blank stare. However, if you provide an accurate template in thin cardboard, any competent glazier should be able to trace around it.

For those who feel that cutting the glass is

completely beyond them, it would be best to have the glazier cut it for you when you buy it. Glass cutting is tricky. It requires firm, confident actions and cannot be done in a tentative or half-hearted way. You may want to practice a few cuts on an old piece of sheet glass to get the feel of scoring the glass. Make sure the practice sheet is clean. Dirt dulls the wheel of the glass cutter, and no one, not even a pro, can do a good job with a dull cutter.

If you do decide to cut the glass yourself, buy a 12-inch square of plate glass and a new glass cutter. Clean the face of the glass. Lay it down on a firm, flat surface upon a few sheets of newspaper and trace the outline of your template on the glass with a china marker or a felt-tipped pen, which will leave a faint but visible line. Alternately, you can put the template under the glass and use it as your guide directly. Lay a good steel straightedge, such as a small carpenter's square, along one of the nine sides of the figure, taking into account the width of the glass cutter.

When cutting glass, draw the little wheel of the cutter toward yourself with a firm, even pressure from one edge of the glass to the other, using the straightedge as a guide, so that it cuts a single, unbroken score line right across the surface of the glass.

Never cut across one score line with a second score line. *Never* saw the glass cutter back and forth. *Never* stop a cut and begin it again. *Never* trace the same cut twice. Each time you make a cut it is a good idea to put a tiny drop of light machine oil on the wheel of the glass cutter to lubricate and clean it.

After making each score line, turn the glass over and tap gently along the bottom with the back of the glass cutter. If you tap too hard, the glass will break, but not where you want it to. Plate glass is too thick to easily break with only your fingers. The best way to divide the glass is to lay it over a straight piece of thick wire—a section of coat hanger is perfect—with the score line up. Align the score line so that it is directly above the wire, which must extend beyond either side of the glass. Holding the main part of the glass down with one hand, press firmly on the up-tilted side of the score line with the heel of your other hand. The wire acts as a fulcrum. The glass should split exactly along the line.

A less dependable method is to lay the score line facing up along the edge of a board and break the glass by pressing down on the projecting section. This is more likely to result in an uneven break, especially if the initial scoring of the glass was poorly done. In either method, take great care not to cut yourself. The glass is actually sharper than a razor. This is particularly important in the final cuts, where you will be dealing with small triangles of glass. Protect your palm with a heavy glove or a pad of burlap.

Repeat the cutting process for each of the nine sides of the nonagon. Remember, never cut across a score line you have previously made in the glass—make each cut separately. If you position the template against one edge of the glass to begin with, you will only need to make eight cuts.

Glass cutting can be one of the most satisfying, or frustrating, experiences of life. In the complete commitment required in the acts of scoring and breaking the glass there is a Zen-like wholeness. Doubt and hesitation must be banished from the mind. Once a cut is begun it cannot be stopped and tried again. It is worth attempting to cut the glass merely to feel this total dedication of the self called upon by this simple manual task.

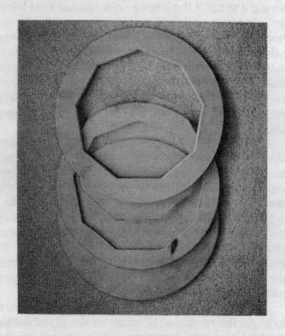

The basic components fo the mirror cut to size. Notice that the upper face-ring has been beveled slightly on the inner edge.

The Frame

The mirror frame is built of three layers of 1/4" plywood laminated together. You will need three one-foot square pieces of 1/4" plywood that are free from knots, gaps or other defects. In cutting these squares be very careful not to splinter the outer layer of the plywood with the saw. It is a good idea to make them slightly larger than 12" on a side to take this splintering into account.

Lay a 12" LP phonograph record (not your favorite) in the middle of *each* plywood square and trace around it. Also trace the center hole, taking care that you keep your pencil at a constant angle relative to the record. It is important that you be able to locate the exact center of the circle.

With a coping saw or other tool cut away the excess wood outside the circle so that you have three identical plywood disks, each one foot in diameter. This can be done with a power table saw using a fine-toothed blade, but it requires a light touch. You want an edge that is not splintered and very close to the circle in order to reduce the amount of sanding required later.

Put one of the disks aside. Using your mathematical compass, draw a circle of 9 1/2" in diameter on one of the remaining disks, and a circle of 9" diameter on the other. It is very important that these circles be centered within the 12" circles you have already traced.

Lay your nine-sided piece of glass within the 9 1/2" circle and trace the shape of the glass with a pencil. Cut out this nonagon using either a coping saw, jigsaw, or chisel. This cut will be hidden when the mirror is assembled, so it can be made a little roughly without hurting the final product.

When you are done you should have a plywood disk 12" in diameter with a nine-sided hole in the center that will snugly hold the piece of plate glass when it is fitted into the plywood disk. The glass and plywood should be nearly the same thickness.

With your protractor, lay out a nonagon in the 9" circle on the remaining disk. You should find this easy to do since by this time you have had a lot of practice. Alternately, you can draw this nonagon on a piece of paper and cut it out to create a template of nine sides based on a 9" circle.

Lay the template within the circle on the plywood disk and trace the figure around it. Cut out this nonagon with a coping saw. This time you must use care in following the line and not splintering the plywood because this cut will frame the face of the finished mirror.

When you have finished making these cuts you will have three 12" plywood disks, one solid, one with a hole in the shape of a nonagon based upon a 9 1/2" circle, and the last with a nine-sided hole based upon a 9" circle. In fact, the distance across these nonagons will be a little less than the diameter of the circles upon which they were formed. (See illustration 6.)

The inner edge of the third disk must be sanded smooth. Wrap a piece of medium grit sandpaper over a flat stick such as a ruler and take the roughness and irregularity off the edge of the smaller nonagon. Take special care that you do not sand the sides too much, or you will destroy the shape. At this stage you can also lay the three disks together and sand away the worst of the irregularities on the outer edge using medium grit paper and a sanding block to keep the edge at right angles to the surface of the disks.

Use fine sandpaper held around a ruler to remove the remaining scratches on the inner edge of the third disk (smaller nonagon). Find the best side of this disk. This will serve as the face of your mirror frame. Gently bevel the upper edges of the planes of the nonagon, but leave the lower edges—the edges that will actually lie touching the face of the glass —with sharp right angles.

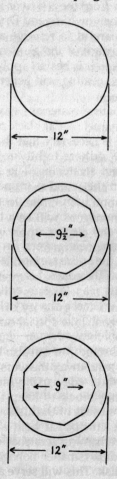

Coating the Glass

Make certain the glass is cleaned of all traces of dust, grease and soap. Wash it with detergent, then run clean water from the tap over its surface until it squeaks under your fingers. Dry it with paper towels, being careful to remove all the lint and fibers. If one surface of the glass has a scratch or other small defect, it is best to apply the coating to this surface. The coating will generally render the scratch invisible.

The best coating material I have found is flat black marine enamel. A flat black rust paint might also be used. It is necessary that the paint be completely opaque, adhere tightly to the glass, and resist friction and scratching. The same paint will also be used on the wooden frame. A pint can is more than enough. I apply the paint with a brush, but there is no reason why it cannot be sprayed on.

Find the worst surface of the glass and lay it facing up on some newspapers. Brush a thick layer of enamel over the entire surface, taking care that it does not drip off the edges. Leave it until it is completely dry. This may take an entire day, or even longer. Marine enamel dries very slowly. When the paint is dry, hold the glass up to a strong light. If it is not yet completely opaque—if you can see the least shadow through the paint—replace the glass on the newspapers and give it a second coat. Two layers of enamel is usually enough, but if the mirror is still not opaque, use three.

You will find that the flat paint appears glossy when viewed through the glass. Examine the glossy surface carefully for any defects. If you have missed a small piece of lint when cleaning the glass, it will show white against the black paint. Scrape it away with a knife and fill the resulting hole with fresh paint.

Placing the Natural Fluid Condenser

After you have applied your last coat of black enamel, and while the paint is still wet, take the powdered mixture of the fluid condenser between your thumb and forefinger and carefully spread it over the back of the mirror upon the wet paint. Make a clockwise inward spiral starting from the outer edge and work in three complete revolutions in to the center of the mirror. The fluid condenser powder should evenly cover the back of the mirror.

This should be done on a Monday night when the Moon is above the horizon and in its waxing phase. It is best if the Moon is full or nearly full, and approaching midheaven.

When the paint dries, it will seal the fluid condenser into the very material of the mirror backing. You may, if you wish, spray a light coat of flat black enamel over the powder to further lock it into place, but I have not found this to be necessary. If you do this, make sure the paint you apply with a brush and the paint you spray are of the same type.

Assembly

Using white carpenter's glue, join the back of the mirror, which is the solid plywood disk, to the middle layer, the disk that will hold the glass inside its nonagon-shaped hole. Make sure you select the smoothest side of the solid disk to face outward. Any defects on the other side will be hidden behind the mirror. Align the two disks so that the meeting grains of the wood cross at a right angle. This will give the finished frame more strength. It is important to clamp the plywood disks all around the edge so there will be no gaps when the glue dries. This will require half a dozen small carpenter's C-clamps. Put blocks of wood between the frame and the jaws of the clamps, or you will indent the soft plywood.

Clamping the back to the middle-ring during the gluing procedure. The recess in the center holds the symbolic fluid condenser and the glass.

After the glue has dried—it is best to leave it overnight—you may position the symbolic fluid condenser into the nonagon pocket of the middle plywood layer with the pentacle of Solomon facing up. Put a few tiny droplets of glue on the edges of the back of the paper where they will not blur the images, and carefully center the symbolic fluid condenser in the hole. The glue will keep it from shifting. Now pull out three hairs from your head by the roots and place them on top of the pentacle. These do not need to be fixed down. The hairs will bind the mirror to you and completely render it your personal instrument. Others who try to use it will not get good results because it will be attuned to your identity.

The symbolic fluid condenser rests within the frame recess. In the center of the purple nonagon is the pentacle of the Moon. The glass has already received its black enamel backing and is ready for the natural fluid condenser.

Lay the glass into the pocket with the coated side down so that it presses against the paper. Then glue over it the third plywood disk, which acts as a retaining ring, positioning it in such a way that the grain which touches the second disk crosses the grain of the second disk at a right angle, or nearly a right angle. Take care not to get any glue on the glass itself. The glue should be applied more thickly toward the outer edge to insure a complete seal with no gaps. Again, clamp the plywood into place and let the glue dry.

It is very important that you do not apply stress to the glass itself in this clamping operation, or you may crack it. Many small C-clamps arranged around the outer edge of the frame will insure a seamless join without flexing the glass. If it happens that the glass is slightly thicker than the plywood you are using, the top retaining ring will be domed slightly after clamping. This is acceptable. If the glass is slightly thinner than the plywood, you may want to place one or more layers of purple blotter under the symbolic fluid condenser to act as a spacer so that the glass does not rattle loosely in the frame. Ideally, the glass and its enamel back, plus the two fluid condensers, should be the same thickness as the middle plywood layer.

Finishing

Cover the entire exposed surface of the glass with a sheet of heavy brown paper and masking tape right to the edge, leaving no gaps where even the smallest part of the glass is exposed. *Do this before you do anything else.* The paper and the tape holding it in place will protect the glass from scratches while you work on the frame itself.

With medium grit sandpaper on a sanding

block—a small block of wood about 5 1/2" x 3 1/2" x 3/4" that acts as a flat support for a quarter sheet of sandpaper—remove the remaining irregularities on the outer edge of the frame. Hold the sanding block at a right angle to the frame until you are certain you have made the frame completely circular. Coarse grit paper should not be necessary, but if there are very deep gouges you may want to begin with it.

Only after the edge of the frame is a perfectly flat circular band should you begin to round it with the sandpaper into a gently curved profile, like the outer edge of a doughnut. You should strive for a degree of rounding that is in visual harmony with the bevel you have already produced on the top inner edge of the upper plywood layer. Use fine sandpaper held loosely in your hand to do the final smoothing of the outer edge. Fine sandpaper on the sanding block should be sufficient to give you a smooth, flat surface on the face and back of the frame, if you have taken care not to scratch the plywood earlier. Remember, always sand back and forth in the same direction as the grain of the wood when sanding flat surfaces. Never use a side-to-side or circular motion.

This sanding operation is tedious but important. Whether it is done well or carelessly will determine the smoothness of the final surface. If there are gaps in the plywood, these must be filled with putty or wood filler. Clean off the sanding dust with a damp rag, and go over the entire frame with fine sandpaper to eliminate any remaining roughness or scratches. Strive for perfection.

With a small brush paint the frame with the same black marine enamel you used on the back of the glass. Begin on the face, then turn the mirror over and set it on a can so that you can do the edge and back. Apply the paint thinly so that it does not pool or run. There is no point in trying to apply it thickly—the bare wood will drink it like a sponge. At least two coats will probably be needed before the laminated layers of the plywood cease to be visible. At this stage you will realize why it is necessary to do a good sanding job, but, of course, it is now too late to go back and correct your mistakes. Let the paint dry thoroughly before applying the next coat.

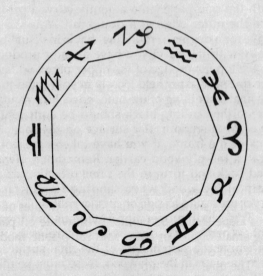

When you have achieved an even, flat velvet surface, you can decorate the frame with occult symbols that contribute to the working of the mirror. These are applied with a fine artist's brush using metallic silver and white paint.

On the front paint the 12 signs of the zodiac.

These should be applied in the mirror opposite of their traditional order, and oriented to be viewed from the perspective of the center of the mirror. Use your protractor to mark out the 12 divisions of the circle on the protective paper masking the glass. It should not be necessary to make any construction lines on the frame itself.

The zodiac is appropriate because it symbolically encompasses the entire world, both heavenly and earthly. Twelve, the number of the zodiac, plus nine, the number of the Moon, equal 21, which is 7 x 3, seven being the number of the traditional planets and three, a lunar number representing the phases of the Moon. Three also represents the three occult worlds—the elementary, celestial, and intellectual—in which the mirror functions.

On the back of the frame in metallic silver, paint a large symbol of the unicursal nonagram, which is the star of nine points drawn with a single interweaving line. Use the more open form of the unicursal nonagram that reflects from every second point, as opposed to the other which reflects from every fourth point.

In the center, place the stylized figure of three linked eyes shown in the diagram. The whites of the eyes alone should be painted with white oil paint. The small bottles of paint sold for plastic models work well enough if the paint is applied thickly.

The nine letters around the outer points of the nonagram are from the Enochian alphabet and constitute the divine name ZIRENAIAD, which translates "I am the Lord your God" (Zir Enay Iad). The letters at the inner points of the nonagram make up the divine name GAHOACHMA, a name of power signifying roughly the same as the Hebrew divine name Eheieh: "I am that I am."

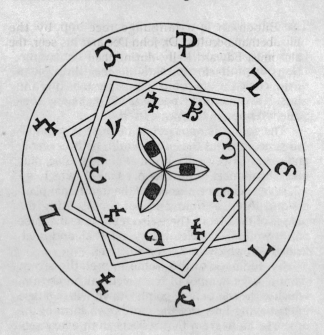

ZIRENAIAD:

GAHOACHMA:

Enochian is a language received by the Elizabethan occultist Dr. John Dee and his seer, the alchemist Edward Kelly, during their communications with discarnate Intelligences through the media of their magic mirror and crystals. It is quite potent magically. Try to copy the shapes of the Enochian letters exactly.

Because this design is so complex, it will be necessary to draw it out on paper and then transfer it to the back of the mirror. On paper, trace a 12" circle using your LP phonograph record and mark the center. Then draw within it another 9" diameter circle with your compass and divide it into nine segments with your protractor, as you have already done several times earlier. Form the unicursal nonagram by drawing a reflecting line to every second point on this inner circle, then double these lines inwardly to thicken them to 1/4". You may wish to interlace the lines of the nonagram as I have done in the diagram.

The three inner eyes are formed by extending three radii, each separated by 120 degrees, toward three angles of the nonagon. Open your compass to 2" and, placing the point on each of these radii in turn, draw three arcs that intersect through the center of the figure. This will define the three eyes. The eyelids may be thickened by connecting the three holes where you set the point of your compass with straight lines, thus creating an equilateral triangle, the sides of which pass vertically through the centers of the eyes. Close the compass to about 1 1/4" and, setting its point along the lines of the triangle, draw arcs above and below each eye to thicken it, so that all arcs intersect at the corners of the eyes. The pupils of the eyes are 3/4" in diameter.

This may sound complicated, but it is really quite simple. However, if you find that you are unable to draw the eyes with your compass, it is perfectly all right to do it freehand using your own artistic judgment.

Tape the perforated mask that bears the outline of the nonagram and the Enochian names of power to the back of the mirror frame, taking care to center it exactly. Spray lightly once or twice over the entire surface of the mask. When you strip the mask away, you will find the outline of the design transferred to the painted back surface in tiny silver dots.

It is a good idea to draw the Enochian letters on the paper as well, so that you will be sure to get them all the same size and evenly spaced around the nonagram. If you make a mistake on paper, you can always erase it.

The design is transferred to the back of the mirror using an ancient fresco technique. Take a needle or pin and carefully outline the entire design by poking holes along its edge. The holes should be separated by no more than 1/4" on straight lines, and 1/8" or less where there are tight curves such as on the letters. Be sure to put a hole at each point of intersection, where the lines of the design cross or touch.

If you do not wish to spend money on a spray can, you can accomplish the same end by dipping a stiff artist's brush, or an old toothbrush, into silver paint and flipping your thumb repeatedly across the stiff bristles to make the paint fly off in a spray. This is messy, but it works.

Cut out the 12" circle with scissors, center it on the back of the mirror and tape it into place. Make sure it lies flat. Be careful not to tape over your pinholes. Use a can of silver spray paint to lightly mist the surface of the paper once or twice. There is no need to lay the paint on thickly. If you do, it will only blur and run. It is best to allow the paint to dry before stripping away the paper mask. You should find a perfect outline of the design on the mirror back in tiny silver dots. If you do not wish to spend money on a can of spray paint, you can do the same thing by spritzing the paint off the end of a stiff artist's brush or a toothbrush with your thumb to create a spray effect.

The nonagram and Enochian letters are done in silver, as are the eyelids of the eyes. The whites of the eyes are done in white oil paint. The centers of the eyes are left black. If your brush happens to stray beyond the lines when painting the figure, you can cover your mistake with flat black enamel.

After you have allowed the design to completely dry, give the entire frame at least two coats of clear high-glass plastic varnish. This will transform the dull satin surface of the paint into a deep black gloss. Solvent-based varnish has a tendency to make the solvent-based metallic silver paint blur, so it is best to use the new water-based plastic varnish.

Only after the last coat of clear plastic has been applied and allowed to dry should you remove the protective brown paper from the face of the mirror. You may have to cut carefully around the inner edge of the frame with a sharp knife to prevent pulling paint off the frame when your remove the tape. If any bits of adhesive remain on the surface of the glass when the masking tape is stripped away, wipe them off with a little paint thinner on a rag.

5

Lunar Charging

Magnetizing the Glass

Before the mirror can be used, it is necessary to align it and make it a conductor, or conduit, of the powers of the Moon. This may be likened to the tuning of a musical instrument before it can be played. The relationships which lie dormant in the two kinds of fluid condensers must be activated, and the condensers charged with lunar potential, which they will then retain for a considerable time the way a battery holds its charge of electrical potential.

This is not a simple mechanical process. It requires the complete involvement of the will and imagination of the owner of the mirror. The mirror does not exist separately from its maker—it is an integral part of the psyche of the person who has crafted it and the person who uses it, ideally the same person. The mirror exists on the physical level, but also on the astral level of the imagination, and the mental level of abstract relationships and archetypal essences. It receives its vitality and identity—the heart of what it does and is—from the highest level; it functions in an observable way on the middle level; and it is anchored and given stability by the lowest level. All three are necessary for the working of the glass.

When the Moon is approaching or has attained

its full face—ideally on the three consecutive nights of each month when the full lunar disk is visible, if all three nights are free from cloud—take the mirror outside when the Moon has nearly reached midheaven, its highest point in the sky. It is best if you can sit comfortably without having to worry about dampness, cold, insects, or other distractions. Sit facing the Moon, and make sure you have an unobstructed view of it.

Look steadily at the Moon and establish an inner link with it. When you feel you have accomplished this, raise the mirror in both your hands and present it to the Moon as you would present an offering at an altar. Be fully aware that you are dedicating the mirror to the powers of the Moon so that it may function with the aid of these powers. Hold the mirror in such a way that its face is directed at the Moon.

Speak this prayer of dedication:

> *Selene of the silver face,*
> *Fill this vessel with thy light;*
> *With arms to act and eyes to see*
> *In secret realms and hidden ways.*

Rest the mirror in your lap or upon a small table so that you can catch the reflection of the Moon in its depths. Do not let go of the mirror; hold it between your hands. Look intently at the image of the Moon in the mirror and begin to recite this chant under your breath:

> *Luna, Diana, Persephone,*
> *Hecate with faces three,*
> *Descend, ascend, and come to me.*

You may make up your own chant if you prefer, but it must be a verse that you can repeat over and over in a circle with only a small portion of your awareness occupied in remembering the words, and it must explicitly call down the powers of the Moon. In the above chant these forces are represented anthropomorphically by goddesses.

As you chant, let the rhythm of the words harmonize with your breaths. Focus your will upon the image of the Moon in the glass, and mentally strengthen and enlarge it. Visualize a silver halo around the Moon extending to the mirror frame like an expanding silver ripple on the surface of a deep, black pool. Draw this energy into the frame with your hands and feel its coolness against your palms and fingertips. Do not let it flow up your arms—keep it concentrated within the mirror.

When the mirror seems to scintillate with a silver glow and you can feel its energy building into a vortex, which will naturally tend to be created by the circular shape, and when you are convinced the mirror can absorb no more of the virtue of the Moon, hold your two hands outstretched with palms down a little above the mirror, and speak this binding incantation:

> *Selene of the starry night,*
> *I bind thy power and thy light*
> *Within this glass before thy sight.*

As you finish, slowly bring your hands together so that they cut the beam of light that extends from the Moon to the surface of the glass. Keep your eyes fixed upon the image of the Moon in the glass, and move your hands in such a way that the circle of the Moon is cut into on each side by the invisible reflection of your hands, reduced to a silver line, and finally blocked altogether. Lower your joined hands, which should be touching along the index fingers, onto the surface of the mirror.

Raise your eyes to the Moon and give a personal thanks for the light you have received, using these or similar words:

> *I thank thee, threefold Hecate,*
> *Goddess of the shining veil,*
> *Goddess of the silver bow,*
> *Goddess of the secret key,*
> *Luna, Diana, Persephone.*

Immediately wrap the mirror in blue or purple silk and take it to its place of keeping. It is not good to try to use the mirror on the same night it is magnetized. The act of charging the mirror and the act of scrying are completely separate. To try to perform one after the other can cause a psychic clashing of gears. The mirror may be used on the following day and any time thereafter.

I recommend recharging the mirror in this manner at least every three months or so if it is to retain its maximum potential. When the mirror is stored in a box of pine inside its silk wrap and not handled by anyone or looked at (which is an astral form of handling), it will keep its lunar charge indefinitely and will be as potent a year later as it was the day you put it away.

A Lunar Collyrium

Get a clear glass bottle that will hold about a quart. The best shape is a decanter or other small-mouthed vessel that can be tightly stoppered. Take this to a flowing spring, stream or river that has uncontaminated water and fill it. In an emergency you can use tap water, but natural fresh water is superior. It really is worthwhile to take the extra effort to go and collect this yourself. Do not use distilled water. This has been processed, filtered and purified until there is no occult virtue left in it.

When you get the water home, drop a pinch of salt into it. Natural rock salt or sea salt is best. Also put into the bottle a medium-sized piece of natural rock crystal. Crystals are relatively easy to obtain these days, thanks to the crystal craze. Try to get one that is clear its entire length and, if possible, one with a natural termination at both ends. Most are simply snapped off at the base.

On a night when the Moon is full, or nearly so, and the sky is clear, take this vessel of water outside and hold it between your hands in the full moonlight. Make sure your fingers do not cast a shadow over the crystal. Speak this incantation under your breath:

> *Selene of the starry night,*
> *Fill this vessel with thy light.*

Visualize a silver glow shining with luminous brightness from the water, concentrating itself within the facets of the rock crystal. Fix your eyes upon the crystal and *will* the moonlight into it. Success of this operation depends on how strongly you will it to happen and how clearly you are able to visualize its realization. Picture a swirling of moonlight spiraling down in a sunwise direction with its focus at the center of the rock crystal.

When you feel that the water and the crystal cannot hold any more lunar virtue, set the vessel down and speak the binding formula you used earlier when charging the mirror:

> *Selene of the starry night,*
> *I bind thy power and thy light*
> *Within this glass before thy sight.*

With your right index finger, inscribe in the air over the vessel an equal-armed circle-cross, while you hold the vessel in your left hand, first the vertical arm, drawing it toward yourself, then the horizontal arm, from left to right, and finally the circle clockwise from the top end of the vertical arm so that it intersects the cross at four points. The circle-cross is drawn flat over the vessel in a plane parallel to the plane of the horizon. Do not make a standing circle-cross.

Wrap the vessel of charged water in a piece of blue or purple silk and put it in a secure place. It should not be recharged. The silk acts as a magical insulation and will keep the lunar virtue contained for months if it is not disturbed. As the water is used up, refill the vessel with fresh water, prepare it and charge it in the same way already described.

The reason for putting a crystal in the water is that crystal is a powerful natural accumulator of lunar virtue. It can store more potential than the water it displaces, even more than the entire vessel, and as the lunar virtue drains out of the water itself over time, it will be replenished from the reservoir in the crystal.

Whenever you use the mirror for scrying, daub a few drops of the charged water upon your eyelids, applying it with the joined index, middle and ring finger of the right hand first to the left eyelid, then the right. Finally, put a few drops on your psychic third eye, the space on your forehead between your eyebrows. This lunar collyrium will heighten your own clairvoyant vision and magnify the power of the mirror. You can use the mirror without the collyrium, but for those who find difficulty in perceiving images in the depths of the glass, the magnetized water will greatly help.

Crystal Fluid Condensers

Natural rock crystal may also be carried or worn on the body in the form of jewelry as an aid in scrying with the mirror. Crystal that has been cut and polished is not as effective. It is best to keep a certain crystal solely for the purpose of scrying in the mirror, and to wear it at no other time. The most useful form of jewelry is a pendant worn on a long silver chain over the heart center. A circlet shaped so that a crystal is positioned on the forehead over the psychic third eye is also useful, but this must be specially made, whereas pendants of natural rock crystal are common in shops and craft displays, and very inexpensive.

If you do make or buy a crystal pendant for the purpose of mirror scrying, be certain to set the crystal in a silver setting and hang it on a silver chain. Use only pure silver. Be careful you do not get stuck with iridium, which jewelers are now trying to dump because of its unpopularity. It was supposed to become the universal substitute for silver a few years ago because it does not tarnish. Unfortunately, it has an ugly look and feel, and people hated it, so there is a lot of it floating around. You can distinguish it from silver by its cold sheen, like stainless steel; silver is warm.

The crystal pendant or other jewelry must be periodically charged with moonlight for the best results. Once every season, or four times a year, is enough. Keep the crystal wrapped in silk or inside a pine box when it is not actually being used for scrying—the same container that holds the mirror is an ideal place. To awaken the power of the crystal, put a few drops of magnetized lunar water on it just before using it. It is best if you wear the crystal in such a way that it touches and is warmed by your bare skin.

6

Preparations

The mirror may be used informally anywhere and any time the mood strikes, or formally within the context of an occult ritual. There are advantages to both methods. An informal use of the mirror involves less preparation, less time and effort expended in peripheral activities. The mirror can be consulted immediately when the need arises. However, many seers find that if the scrying is treated in a casual way, the results also tend to be ordinary. When the process of scrying is elevated as the centerpiece of a formal magical ritual, the significance of the visions seen in the depths of the mirror is heightened.

There is another reason for using a formal ritual. Ritual opens and shuts the door to your unconscious, allowing a distinct separation between magical work and everyday living. When you enter a ritual, you leave mundane problems and cares temporarily behind you. When you leave the ritual, you similarly turn away from the unpredictable, miraculous astral world of spirits and elemental forces. The ritual circle acts as a border that separates the commonplace from the magical, and it is desirable that they be kept apart to some extent as intrusion of each world can inhibit effective functioning in the other. You do not wish to be troubled by spirits while you are trying to calculate your income tax; neither do you wish to be worrying about tax problems when you are seeking magical experiences.

In a sense, all uses of the mirror, even the most informal, will be ritualized. The seer will proceed in a set way, following a predetermined series of steps. Those that seem to help will be repeated invariably; those that appear to serve no purpose will be dropped. Soon a well-defined pattern of ritual actions will manifest itself and become a necessary prerequisite to each consultation of the mirror. It is up to the scryer whether these set actions shall be trivial and accidental, or consciously linked at the outset with the occult energies of gods and spirits.

In most cases the person consulting the mirror will be alone. Elaborate external rituals are of limited value to solitary occultists. They are designed to create a dramatic effect within a group, the members of which use the ritual actions to draw meaning from one another. Solitary occultists are best served by internal rituals that have a minimum of physical elements. Outwardly, they should be kept simple. Inwardly, they may be more involved.

If the mirror is to be used seriously, not as a toy, a place must be set aside specifically for scrying and magical work. This is usually called the ritual temple, but this term is needlessly grand. A small room in your house, or even a corner of a room, is sufficient for mirror working, which is largely performed in the astral temple of the imagination. The place should be kept clean and uncluttered, the furnishings neutral. Avoid jarring elements such as bright colors or bold patterns that tend to distract the eye.

A small table to support the mirror, preferably

with a single column and a round top, and a plain wooden chair are the only furniture needed. If you are accustomed to sitting on the floor, either cross-legged (*sukhasana*) or in one of the yoga asanas such as the *siddhasana*, *padmasana*, or *virasana*, or Japanese style (*vajrasana*), even this furniture may be replaced by a mat 3 x 6 feet in size. The mirror may be set upon the floor or held in the hands.

You may find it preferable, as I do, to work with the mirror in an upright position at eye level about three feet from your face. A small support of the type used to display ornamental plates or photographs on tables will hold the mirror at a convenient angle. It is better if the mirror is tilted away from your face so that you will not be distracted by your own reflection in the glass. This tilting will naturally happen if the mirror is placed flat on a table in front of you or in one of the angled plate holders.

I prefer to have the mirror close enough to touch because it has been designed to a human dimension to serve as a personal instrument. Strictly speaking, there is no reason why the mirror will not function perfectly well at a greater distance, even across the room. Its relative area would still be larger than that of many magic mirrors used in ancient times, such as natural rock crystal or the nail of the thumb.

The magic place should be cleaned regularly and never allowed to become untidy. Chaos without reflects chaos within. It is best to use the place only for occult purposes, but where this is impossible, at least the furniture—table, mirror stand, chair, mat—should be set aside solely for magical work.

The physical temple is only the foundation for

the real temple of magic which exists on the astral plane, constructed and furnished by the imagination. This may be as simple or as ostentatious as you wish. It may be a mental recreation of a physical place, or a setting that is completely imaginary, drawn from myth, fiction or your own dreams and desires. Each time you consult the mirror in the physical temple you must mentally enter your astral temple, and during the use of the mirror, maintain a sense of your complete presence there, as much as possible divorcing your sensory awareness from your material surroundings.

It is best to settle on the nature of your astral temple early and begin the lengthy process of building it on the astral plane as soon as possible. This is done by visualizing as clearly as you are able each astral feature or furnishing in turn, trying as best you can to actually enter the astral temple and abide there during your rituals. You will discover that it is as necessary to construct the astral temple bit by bit with labor over time as it would be if you actually built it with your hands using wood and stone. The astral temple can be changed, but this is a serious matter and should not be done lightly, any more than you would change the house you live in on a whim.

A light diet made up mainly of vegetables and whole grains, such as brown rice, whole wheat and rolled oats, that uses little red meat and avoids entirely fried or greasy foods will greatly enhance the clairvoyant power. This is because the body has a hard time processing grease and meat, particularly when these are eaten in large quantities and all its energies are concentrated on digestion. When you sit down to scry in the mirror, you will find yourself listening to the churning of your stomach and the workings of your intestinal tract.

Eat light, nourishing foods in moderate amounts, and do not eat anything for four or five hours before scrying so that your stomach will have a chance to at least partially empty itself. You do not need to starve, only to regulate your diet. Occasional light fasting, for a period of 24 hours or so, will be beneficial. Experiment with different foods and meal schedules and you will quickly discover which bring the best results.

Something as basic as diet may at first consideration seem a trivial concern in the matter of magic, but, on the contrary, it is extremely important. Any way you can alter your physical body has an immediate effect upon your astral and mental bodies, an effect more profound than any amount of vague wishful thinking and empty, hypocritical resolves. When you change your physical body, you have actually *done* something. It is all too easy when working in the astral to pretend to have done something, or to do something and the next moment undo it.

Breathing exercises in the morning just after rising also awaken the clairvoyant power. These can be repeated prior to scrying to fill the body with a charge of *prana*, the occult vitalizing energy of the air.

Sit comfortably with your hands on your thighs. Empty your lungs completely. Slowly expand your diaphragm downward and fill with air the lower third of your chest cavity. When the bottom of your lungs is filled, shift your attention up to your solar plexus and fill the central portion of your chest. Finally, shift your awareness to the very top of your lungs and raise your shoulders by pressing your hands lightly against your thighs, inflating the upper third of your chest.

Hold this air comfortably for about five seconds. There should be no strain, either in emptying or filling the lungs. Exhale in reverse sequence, first lowering your shoulders, then emptying the central part of your chest, and at last expelling all the air from your lower lungs with the aid of your diaphragm. Hold your lungs empty for a similar duration of about five seconds. Take care not to close or lock your throat either when holding the air out or in.

The author indrawing a lunar breath through the left nostril.

Each inhalation should take a maximum of about 15 seconds—five for each stage—and each exhalation 15 seconds, so that each complete breath, including retentions, lasts at most about 40 seconds. With practice the stages may be lengthened, but you should never try to stretch the intervals beyond your endurance. If you find that 40 seconds is too long for a breath, it is perfectly permissible to shorten the intervals. You can hurt yourself by trying to push your lungs beyond their capacity. This will achieve nothing but a persistent cough, an ache in your chest and a ringing in your ears. Strive for a smooth, effortless flow of air in and out of your lungs so that the three stages merge imperceptibly into one another.

As you draw air in, visualize it glowing with silver lunar virtue, and as you expel it, visualize the lunar magnetism remaining within your body and circulating to your eyes and head. If you wish, you may use alternate nostril breathing and draw the air in through your left, lunar nostril while you seal your right, solar nostril with the thumb of your right hand; then exhale through your right nostril while sealing the left nostril with the tips of your ring and little finger. The index and middle fingers of the right hand, which are not used, are kept folded into the palm.

This kind of lunar breathing is very intense. It will create an imbalance of lunar potential within your body and, therefore, should only be done for a few minutes prior to scrying in order to further energize your clairvoyant faculty. In general practice, lunar and solar breaths—inhalation through the left and right nostrils, respectively—should alternate.

It is suggested that you bathe or shower (actually a bath is preferable) before each scrying session. As you cleanse yourself physically, hold the awareness in your mind that you are also cleansing away the corruption and accumulated detritus from your sense of self. Wash yourself clean for the same purpose you wash a window—so the light can shine through it unhindered. Wash yourself for the reason you wipe off a blackboard with a damp rag—so that new information can be recorded there and clearly read.

By the same token, you must keep your magic mirror free from fingerprints, dust and dirt. Not that these visually hinder the psychic images seen in its depths, but because they symbolically impede the brightness and clarity of the visions. The spirits that aid in the transmission of these visions perceive dirt on the mirror surface in its astral manifestation as a kind of psychic occlusion or shadow. A little glass cleaner sprayed on a paper towel will keep the mirror shining. Take care you do not apply so much cleaner that it seeps into the back of the glass and damages the fluid condensers.

If you are to derive the maximum benefit from using the mirror, you must keep a careful record of your scrying sessions and any other uses to which the mirror may be put. A large, loose-leaf binder is the easiest way to organize this magical diary, sometimes referred to as a "book of shadows." With a binder you can take out a sheet if you make a mistake and replace it with a new sheet.

Record the date, time, weather, place, phase of the Moon, purpose, and your general physical and emotional state before beginning. If you employ a ritual framework to focus the projected magical action or the received divination, outline its structure. Also make a note of any anomalous or significant occurrences around the time of the scrying, such as accidents, coincidences, unexplained events, unexpected meetings or disputes, related dreams, and so on.

Briefly, but in as much detail as necessary so as not to miss anything, record what you perceive in the mirror. This may not be actual images. Sometimes only colors or vapors appear, but these possess their own meanings and may be interpreted in relation to the purpose of the scrying. It is important that you record everything, even what seems trivial, because the significance of an image may not reveal itself for days or weeks after you have seen it. Magic has no respect for the laws of cause and effect.

Later, if something happens that triggers your memory, you can check back in your record and see if a synchronicity exists. A record kept over a period of months or years can also reveal your natural cycles of clairvoyance, which may be linked to your environment, pattern of activity, the seasons of the year, or even the astrological configuration of the heavens. If you neglect the diary, you will never be able to investigate why you are able to see more clearly in the mirror on some days than on others.

The accompanying worksheet may serve as a useful guide. Type it up on a single sheet of paper, leaving plenty of room to record the actual vision seen in the glass, photocopy several dozen duplicates, punch holes along their left edges, and put them into a binder. Keep the original sheet as your master, and take more photocopies from it as you need them.

Magic Mirror Worksheet

Date: Time: Lunar phase:

Place:

Weather:

Physical state:

Mental state:

Purpose:

Ritual framework:

Scrying:

Synchronous events:

Conclusions:

7

Ritual Framework

The ritual described below serves to cleanse the ritual place, banish unwanted discordant influences, and invite the presence of desirable harmonious influences. It is simple and brief and may be performed in a few minutes prior to all magical work with the mirror, whether this involves scrying, astral travel, spirit invocation or projection of the will.

Before beginning, bathe and put on loose comfortable clothing. You may wish to have a special robe or other garments exclusively for magical work. It is best if your feet are bare. If you cannot bathe, at least wash your hands and face with the clear intention of cleansing yourself to receive fresh, new impressions. Take the mirror from its place of keeping and solemnly unwrap the silk covering. Face south, kiss the edge of the frame over the sign of the zodiac under which you were born, and speak this dedication:

> *I dedicate this instrument to the service of the Light; may it never be defiled.*

Put the mirror upon its table in the south of the ritual place, either flat on the table or upright in its holder. On the left of the mirror set a black candle in a small brass or silver holder. On the right of the mirror set a white candle. Light the candles, first the black, then the white, using the same flame for both. Dim the room lights so that the only illumination comes from the candles.

Stand in a relaxed way in front of the mirror table facing south. If you are using a chair for scrying, it should be placed out of the way and a few feet behind you in the north. Otherwise, stand upon your meditation mat. Take 13 deep, cleansing breaths, consciously drawing into your body the luminous silver virtue of the Moon from the air. If you wish, you may use left nostril breathing on each inhalation and exhale through the right nostril, alternately closing each with the thumb and last two fingers of your cupped right hand.

Raise your arms in a gesture of invocation, looking up at an angle to infinity. Speak this cleansing prayer:

> Have mercy upon me, O God, blot out
>   my transgressions;
>
> Wash me thoroughly from mine iniq-
>   uity, and cleanse me from my sins;
>
> Purge me with hyssop, and I shall be
>   clean;
>
> Wash me, and I shall be whiter than
>   snow;
>
> Create in me a clean heart, O God,
>   and renew a right spirit within me:
>
> Thou who art the Crown,

And the Kingdom;

The Power,
And the Glory;
And the Law Everlasting;

Amen.

As you say "Crown," lay your left hand over your heart and touch your brow with the index finger of your right hand; as you say "Kingdom," touch your groin; as you say "Power," touch your left shoulder; as you say "Glory," touch your right shoulder; as you say "Law Everlasting," touch the back of your left hand over your heart center and point directly in front of your body; and as you say "Amen," raise your right index finger and point directly overhead.

Keep your left hand on your heart center and touch it again with your right index finger, drawing out of your heart center through your right arm a thread of white spiritual fire. Point in front of you and project this fire from your index finger into the air as you slowly turn sunwise on your own axis, so that you inscribe in the astral world a ring of white fire that floats upon the air and surrounds you at the level of your heart. Speak the words:

> *I project this circle of flaming light*
> *from my center of being. Let no evil or*
> *discordant influence enter into this*
> *ring nor abide within its boundary.*

You may project this circle of fire to any diameter you wish, but nine feet is appropriate for lunar magic. Do not worry if there is a wall or piece of furniture close to you—the fiery circle is not obstructed by material objects.

It is important that you develop your powers of astral vision until you can clearly see in your inner eye this flaming ring and feel its radiance, which is cool rather than warm, and hear it flicker as it burns. Treat it as a real barrier. If you do not, it will never be a barrier to anything on any level, and you might as well not bother making it. When you wish to leave the circle, draw it in along your left arm through your extended left index finger, your right hand over your heart. Begin at the south and turn against the course of the Sun.

In an emergency, such as a sudden interruption or an alarm, you can draw the circle back into your center all at once by closing it down to an infinitely tiny point within your heart, but this is not recommended in regular magical work. It is best to indraw the circle in the reverse order of steps by which you projected it.

As you stand within the circle, abstract your mind away from your material surroundings and imagine that you are on a high place at night that is bare except for your magical instruments and illuminated solely by the candles on the table and the flaming light of the magic circle. This is the true magical place where you will work all your rituals. In time, as you grow familiar with it, you may create and furnish it in any manner that strikes your fancy. In the beginning, keep it simple.

Over the mirror in the air at the level of your heart, draw a standing equilateral triangle, its point up, with flaming red fire. Begin at the top point and project the fire from your heart center as you trace the triangle with your right index finger in a clockwise direction. The triangle should be visualized as floating in the air above the table, about three feet long on each side. Speak the words:

> *By the power of Fire*
> *I cleanse this circle.*

Again using your right index finger, draw an equilateral triangle with its point down in blue flame so that it interlocks with the upright red triangle. Begin it at the bottom point and project it also in a clockwise direction. Speak the words :

> *By the power of Water*
> *I cleanse this circle.*

Draw a circle in yellow flame around the interlocked triangles so that it touches them at their points. Begin at the top of the circle and proceed clockwise. Speak the words:

> *By the power of Air*
> *I cleanse this circle.*

Draw a square of green fire around the circle so that it touches the circle, beginning it at its upper left corner and proceeding clockwise. Speak the words:

> *By the power of Earth*
> *I cleanse this circle.*

Place your palms together in a prayer gesture over your heart. Hold this symbol of a hexagram within a circle within a square clearly in your mind for several seconds. Try to maintain and be aware of all four colors at the same time. Now separate your hands and extend them on either side of your body as though pushing something apart. As you do this, visualize the symbol of the elements breaking apart, each piece of it moving to one of the four quarters of the circle.

The red upright triangle goes to the south, where it floats against the magic circle at heart level; the blue inverted triangle goes to the west on your right side; the yellow circle goes to the north behind you; and the green square goes to the east on your left side. Allow these four symbols to be dissolved and absorbed into the flame of the magic circle, so that they momentarily color each quarter section of it with their own colors. Then let the circle flame pure white once again.

Hold your arms straight out at either side so that your body forms a great cross. Visualize a great pillar of red in the south just *outside* the circle, extending up and down into infinity. Speak the words:

> Before me Michael,
> Lord of Fire,
> Ruler of the South.

Visualize a great pillar of yellow light outside the circle behind you in the north, but do not turn your head to look at it—picture it in your mind. Speak the words:

> Behind me Raphael,
> Lord of Air,
> Ruler of the North.

Picture a blue pillar beyond the circle in the west rising infinitely up through the sky and falling infinitely down into the Earth. Speak the words:

> *On my right Gabriel,*
> *Lord of Water,*
> *Ruler of the West.*

Visualize a pillar of green light beyond the circle in the east. Speak the words:

> *On my left Uriel,*
> *Lord of Earth,*
> *Ruler of the East.*

Hold a clear awareness of these four pillars of colored light as you stand with your arms spread wide. Speak the words:

> *The Four surround me,*

Raise your arms at an angle on either side, palms up, and visualize red fire rising from each of your open hands. Speak the words:

> *Fire above,*

Lower your arms at an angle on each side, palms down, and visualize blue water streaming from your fingers like rain. Speak the words:

> *Water below,*

Bring your palms together over your heart in a prayer gesture and say:

> *I am the heart of the Four,*
> *I am the center of my universe.*

Visualize a cross of white light formed by three beams that meet at right angles in your heart center. One beam runs vertically through your body. Another runs under your shoulders from east to west. The third beam extends through your chest between your joined hands from south to north.

Raise your joined hands and press the lower segment of your two thumbs into the higher part of your forehead where it domes outward. Speak the words:

> *So let it be.*

You may let your hands fall to your sides. Now is the time to clearly express your purpose. Begin with this formula :

> *This ritual is conducted for the pur-*
> *pose...*

State as concisely as possible why you are performing the ritual. If you are going to scry in the mirror, say:

> *This ritual is conducted for the pur-*
> *pose of scrying in the spirit vision.*

Anoint your left eyelid, your right eyelid, and your brow with three drops of the lunar collyrium using the joined index, middle and ring fingers of your right hand. With the index finger inscribe a vortex in the air over the mirror quite close to the surface of the glass, forming a clockwise inward spiral of three turns. Visualize lunar virtue swirling down to impregnate the surface of the glass. Speak the words:

> *Selene of the starry night,*
> *Fill this vessel with thy light.*

Seat yourself upon your chair or mat and begin the work you intend, whether it is scrying, spirit communication, or some other task. The preceding steps create a consecrated space into which occult power may be gathered and retained, and within which you may feel free from disturbance or threat by any discarnate awareness.

It may seem complex, but once you have gone through the steps a few times you will realize that the whole preliminary ritual may be performed in just a few minutes. I am inclined to call it an Establishing Ritual, because it establishes your sacred space and your reason for being there.

Make your gestures fluid as you pass from step to step so that they merge into one another to form a graceful whole. In a similar way, merge the mental actions so that they flow together in your mind. The greater part of the ritual occurs in the astral realm. The physical movements are really only an aid to creating the true ritual in the imagination.

After the main part of your business is concluded, give thanks to your personal conception of the highest Deity for the successful fulfillment of the ritual. Do this even if you think the ritual may have been flawed or spoiled by some error. If you are scrying, it is especially appropriate to give thanks to the goddess of the Moon, Selene:

I give thanks to thee, Shining
Goddess,
For the fulfilling of this ritual pur-
pose.

With your right index finger, make a cross of equal arms over the surface of the mirror, drawing the vertical arm down and toward you, the horizontal arm sunwise from left to right, then enclose the cross in a circle. Visualize this symbol flaming with white light on the surface of the mirror and speak the words:

Selene of the starry night,
Seal this vessel with thy light.

Arise and stand facing the south, hands joined in a gesture of prayer over your heart. Mentally extinguish the four pillars of elemental light at the quarters of the circle, saying:

Guardians of the four ways,
I give thanks to thee for thy service;
Depart in peace, and fare you well.

Extend your arms to either side with your fingers opened wide in a warding off gesture, and mentally send out a circular wave of power from your heart center to push back any spirits who may have been attracted by the activities of your ritual. Speak the words:

All spirits drawn to this ritual circle,
depart this place!
Go! For you have no lawful business

here.
Yet go in peace, and fare thee well.

With your right palm over your heart center, extend your left index finger and mentally indraw the circle of white fire, beginning at the south and rotating on your own axis counterclockwise, which is against the course of the Sun. As you do this, say:

> *I indraw this flaming circle to my*
> *center of being, and return this*
> *chamber to its former state.*

Raise your hands together high over your head with your index fingers touching and draw in the air a great oval with your index fingers on either side of your body, mentally extending it so that it encases your entire body in an egg of white radiance. As you do this, speak the words:

> *May the grace of the One God*
> *Empower and protect me,*

Place your left hand on your heart and inscribe the great cross on your body as you did before with your right index finger, saying:

> *Who art the Crown,* (brow)
> *And the Kingdom;* (groin)
> *The Power,* (left shoulder)
> *And the Glory;* (right shoulder)
> *And the Law Everlasting;* (heart and*
>   south)
>
> *Amen.* (heavens)

Place your hands together in a gesture of prayer over your heart and say:

This ritual is well and truly fulfilled.

Raise your hands to your brow so that the lower segments of your thumbs touch its domed upper part, saying:

So let it be.

Let your hands fall to your sides.

You may now extinguish the candles, first the white candle on the right side, then the black one on the left, and reverently wrap the mirror in its silk insulator. Take a few moments to relax your mind and create an inner calm, then record in your magical diary any visions, impressions, sensations, ideas, or physical events you may have experienced during the ritual.

8

Scrying

Scrying is a natural talent that can, with practice and hard work, be developed. As is true of any gift, to some it will come very easily, while others will never be very good at it despite all their efforts. The great John Dee, the most notable English occultist since Merlin, was a dismal failure as a seer. He employed several scryers to look into his various magic mirrors and describe what they saw, the most successful of whom was Edward Kelly.

Children make the best seers. The traditional explanation is that they are unpolluted by sexual desire. Perhaps for a similar reason the virgin priestesses of Greece and Rome often acted as oracular mediums for the gods. Pregnant women and widows are also said to be clairvoyant. If we follow the same logic, this is presumably because a pregnant woman is temporarily infertile, and therefore nonsexual, while a widow, at least in olden times, was thought to bury her desire with her husband. Extrapolating this premise, we might expect celibate priests, nuns and women past the age of childbearing—"old maids"—to be susceptible to visions, and indeed these groups report an unusual number of occult contacts and perceptions, which are commonly attributed to hysteria arising from suppressed sexuality.

Physiologically, the best seers are said to be those with dark eyes set wide apart beneath a high brow, dark brown hair and swarthy skin. Psychologically, they are intelligent and sensitive persons with strong imaginative powers, high ideals, and a dreamy disposition. that often causes them to appear abstracted from their surroundings. Genetically, certain races appear to possess superior clairvoyant abilities. Celts make better seers than Germans; southern Europeans are generally better than northern Europeans. There are, however, many notable exceptions to these general rules. The Swedish mystic Emanuel Swedenborg was an extraordinarily gifted visionary seer, and he scarcely fits into any of the above categories.

It is possible to increase the power of natural clairvoyance through exercises designed to turn off, for a time, the rational censor of the mind. These exercises, which involve conscious visualizations, clarify and strengthen visionary images so that they do not melt away like snowflakes the instant that awareness touches them. Just as average people wake up as soon as they become aware that they are dreaming, so untrained scryers, the moment they consciously recognize that they are receiving a vision, banish it. Consciousness acts like a powerful laser and sears away the fragile gossamer of astral images even as it illuminates them.

If you have ever searched the night sky for a faint star, you know that when you look directly at it, the star vanishes, but when you look slightly to one side, you can see it only so long as you do not actually look at it. The moment your awareness draws your eye directly to the star, it fades into the velvet blackness of the night. The reason for this is physiological—the central portion of your retina, through use, is less light sensitive than surrounding portions. But it is an exact physical model for what takes place during scrying when you focus your consciousness analytically upon a vision in the mirror.

These exercises will increase your control over the ray of your consciousness so that you may bring it near enough to an image to be aware of it and remember it, but not so close that you destroy it by dissecting it analytically.

Exercise I

As you lie in bed at night before falling asleep, visualize an object. Actually construct it in your mind, examining it from all angles, turning it over, opening it up and looking inside it, putting it back together, exactly as you might with a sophisticated computer program. If you lose the image, simply go back and pick up where you let it slip away. Continue this until you drift into sleep, or if you find that it is keeping you awake, stop after half an hour or so.

You may discover that after you have been performing this exercise intensely for a time the right side of your head will feel cool on top. Do not be frightened. This indicates an increased flow of blood to this portion of your brain. In order for you to develop a visual faculty, certain physiological changes must take place in your brain, just as when you exercise for a certain sport your body changes and develops in very specific ways. In fact, there exist certain discarnate Intelligences whose job it is to regulate and manage these physical changes, and one of their main tasks is to insure that no physical damage is done to the central nervous system.

In my own exercises I employ geometric shapes. First I start with a dimensionless point, then extend it on either side into an infinite line, next open the line into an infinite plane, then bisect the plane at right angles with a second plane, thereby defining a line at intersection, then bisect the two planes at right angles with a third plane, thereby defining a point. I go on to construct various geometric solids and modify them in different ways.

You do not need to use geometry. You can visualize an apple, a pencil, a toaster, a hairpin —anything you know the appearance of inside and out. Try to create the texture of the object as well as the image.

Exercise II

Face a wall or curtain that does not offer any particular point of focus for the eye. If you lie on your bed, you can look at the ceiling. As clearly as you are able, visualize the inside of a house or other building where you have been in the past, a place you know quite well. The house of a distant relative you may have frequently visited in your childhood is good, or a summer house. It does not matter whether the house still exists. Create it in your mind.

Imagine yourself passing through the front door into the hallway or living room. From the depths of your memory bring forth the feel of the floor under your feet, the texture of the door handle, the smell, the ticking of the clock or creak of floorboards. Walk slowly from room to room. Touch the familiar furnishings. Go into the bedrooms, the kitchen, the bathroom, and try to re-create in a concrete way as many features of the place as you can recall. As you pass from room to room through this house of memory, objects will evoke other objects. You may be surprised at how complete a sensory picture you are able to construct.

It is not necessary to close your eyes, and, in fact, better if you leave them open. Do not make a futile effort to actually see the place—try to abstract your mind and separate it from the uninteresting image coming in through your eyes. You will continue to see the wall or ceiling, but your attention will shift to the image you are creating in your imagination.

Exercise III

Seat yourself comfortably and call up in your mind's eye the face of someone you know quite well. Try to see the whole face as you shift your attention from detail to detail, from the corner of the mouth to the arc of the brow, the shape of the ear to the line of the jaw, just as you would if the person were actually seated before you. You can use the face of a long-time friend, a departed relative, an old teacher, so long as you are thoroughly familiar with its features.

When you have completely re-created the face, animate it. Remember the habitual mannerisms and expressions of the person, their smile, the way they raise their eyebrows, purse their lips, tilt their head, and so on.

Finally, recall the voice of the person, both its tone and its inflections, the rhythms of speech, the expressions and choice of words, the accent. Carry on a simple conversation with the person in your mind, and try to actually hear and see the person answering. It does not matter what the conversation is about. The important thing is that you actually experience the individual in your imagination, not merely pretend to see and hear them. There is a difference between these two acts, which is the difference between functioning in the astral and merely remembering.

Again, you need not actually see the person with your physical vision for the exercise to be a success, so long as your awareness is shifted from the sensory message of your eyes and ears to the re-created sights, sounds and feelings of your imagination.

These three exercises, if performed regularly with variations to prevent tedium, will quickly develop a strong visual imagination in those who have the least innate talent for scrying. The exercises may be done between attempts at using the mirror. Practice is the key. You are not trying to memorize a particular piece of information, but are awakening an intuitive faculty. Scrying is like riding a bicycle. No matter how eloquently an expert cyclist describes the process, you will be unable to ride yourself until you have experienced what it is like to balance on two wheels and tumble to the ground.

The images seen in the mirror do not enter your eyes in the form of light waves. The part of your mind that is clairvoyant is stimulated by the use of the mirror, which acts upon it as a symbolic key to open it. The clairvoyant faculty then gathers and coordinates information in ways that do not involve the mediation of your five senses. Since you are unable to understand anything that does not reach your consciousness as sights, sounds, feelings, tastes and smells, this clairvoyant part of you must translate the information it has gathered into sensory information.

If this were not done, you would never be aware that information had been gathered in the first place. And undoubtedly, there is in every person an inherent clairvoyant faculty constantly at work gathering information, but the conscious mind remains cut off from it except under unusual circumstances—great stress of an emotional or physical kind, or deliberate efforts to perceive and channel it such as you are learning from this book.

Since the primary sense is sight and the mirror is a visual instrument, the information gathered by the unconscious is translated into the metaphor of visual images, which reach the consciousness with varying degrees of clarity and congruity. Someone with a limited skill in scrying may see only hazy flashes or shadows, whereas a person with great skill will perceive connected visions with all the lucidity of a cinematic picture.

The important point is that with constant practice and the use of the exercises herein described, you can develop a clairvoyant faculty that is not visual, not even sensory, but which manifests itself in visions, because this is the only way you are able to gain awareness of it.

My grandfather was an accomplished seer. He used tea leaves, cards and a glass crystal ball. To hold the ball, he constructed a cubical box about 12 inches in every dimension that was painted a flat black inside, like the inner chamber of a camera. When scrying, he would lean close to the ball, which rested upon its wooden base inside the opened box, and cover his entire head and shoulders with a black velvet cloth, as the old photographers used to do. This excluded the light totally.

He could not see the crystal at all. Yet he achieved truly remarkable visions, many of which were verified by subsequent physical events.

The visions observed in the mirror are not necessarily direct representations of actual events. If you see a person being shot, for example, it may mean that person has been, is being, or will be shot in exactly that way, or it may mean the person has or will be "shot down" in a figurative sense. It may even be a dramatic metaphor presented for your interpretation that has nothing whatsoever to do with the person, who is merely an actor drafted by your unconscious mind to help portray a particular message.

When you are scrying, you can generally sense by the immediacy of the experience whether a vision is literal or metaphorical. This is something that only comes with practice. Understand that if you happen to see the end of the world in your mirror, it does not necessarily follow that life will cease on planet Earth. However, such a vision may have great significance within your own life.

The initial experiences and sensations of scrying are more or less the same for everyone, although these have been described in various ways by different writers. As you stare constantly at the center of the glass, it will gradually brighten to a misty grey. This light will increase and decrease in intensity for a while as you alternately focus awareness upon it and let it slip to the background of your attention. The grey mist will seem to swirl or billow. This has led to it being described as clouds, smoke and shadows, but it is obvious that everyone who scrys is seeing very much the same phenomenon.

After the initial brightening, colors will manifest themselves. These are quite intense and change rapidly, merging and dissolving from one to another. More than one color will not be visible at any one time except during the brief period of the actual color change, when two colors may be visible in different parts of the glass at the same instant.

The colors are pastel in nature. I have noticed lemon yellow, lime green, chalk blue, pink, and purple-violet. They tend to shift rapidly, each persisting only for a few seconds before being supplanted by the next one.

There is a conventional symbology associated with these preliminary appearances which John Melville gives in his *Crystal Gazing and Clairvoyance*. I will reproduce the information here:

Conventional Color Meanings

White clouds	auspicious
Black clouds	inauspicious
Violet, Green, Blue clouds	coming joy, a good omen
Red, Orange, Yellow clouds	coming grief, sickness, loss, betrayal, an evil omen
Ascending clouds	yes to a question
Descending clouds	no to a question
Clouds on the left	actual representations

Clouds on the right	symbolic representations
Clouds moving to the left	disinterest and withdrawal of spirits
Clouds moving to the right	interest and presence of spirits

The left and right mentioned are the left and right of the scryer. The appearance of descending clouds occurs when the colors form first at the edges and close in to the center. When the colors form first at the center and move out to the edges, the clouds appear to rise up from the depths of the mirror. It should be understood that the colors come and go in large patches on the mirror surface and flow across it rapidly, like billows of colored dye in water.

Although personally I set little store by these stock interpretations, once you have learned and accepted them, your unconscious can use them as a kind of shorthand language to communicate with your awareness, and they can come to acquire conventional meaning while they possess none inherently, just as the word "dog" has no greater essential meaning than the word "nxlz," but has acquired meaning through its use.

Colors do have natural meanings, meanings not agreed upon but simply accepted below the conscious level. I prefer to interpret the mirror according to these natural meanings. It will be seen by comparing the correspondences below with those already given that a certain amount of overlap exists, which is to be expected. It would take perverse genius to devise a conventional set of correspondences completely at variance with Nature:

Natural Color Correspondences

White clouds good, truth, revelation, purity, joy, beginning, spirituality

Black clouds evil, secrets, lies, strife, despair, death, ending

Yellow clouds playfulness, childishness, prosperity, charm, health, gifts, spontaneous art

Purple clouds sickness, dreams, mental problems, imbalance, physical matters

Red clouds anger, strife, lust, action, brutality, command, the will, masculine energy

Green clouds desire, physical growth, love, vitality, envy, display, Nature

Blue clouds	judgment, serenity, ending of disputes, legal settlements, peace, feminine energy
Orange clouds	science, learning, the professions, employment, purposeful activity
Violet clouds	intuitions, occult matters, communications with spirits
Clouds on the left	material, manifest, feminine
Clouds on the right	ideal, mental, masculine
Clouds moving left to right	approach, concentration of forces or spirits
Clouds moving right to left	withdrawal, dispersal of forces or spirits
Clouds rising	revelation
Clouds falling	concealment

Left to right is the way of the Sun across the heavens, the natural path followed by spiritual power when it descends upon the microcosm. Right to left indicates the reverse, the dispersal of that power back into the macrocosm. Left is not so much evil as it is material, and, therefore, non-spiritual. For a more comprehensive treatment of the meanings and relationship of the colors, I strongly urge the reader to study Chapter 33 of my work *The New Magus* (available from Llewellyn Publications, St. Paul, MN).

The most difficult moment in scrying is the transition between the changing colors upon the surface of the mirror and actual images—difficult in the sense of less frequently attained, because no amount of straining, staring or concentrating the will can hasten it. Just the reverse is true. If you strain, you will never achieve the transition. It is necessary to create a reflective state of mind in which the consciousness remains in the background, reduced to the role of passive observer.

The image will form in the center of the glass. At first, it will likely be quite small and distant, as though you are looking at it through the wrong end of a telescope, but if you are able to refrain from seizing upon it with your awareness, it will gradually strengthen and become larger until it fills the greater portion of the glass. If, on the other hand, you grab onto it with your mind, it will dissolve like smoke.

The images in the mirror may be of two types, detached or involving:

Detached images unfold like a motion picture. The seer is an observer and does not interact with the vision in any way. The beings represented in the vision remain totally unaware that they are being watched. Most early success in scrying, and most visions that involve existing physical settings and living people, are of this kind. The majority of all scrying is detached.

Involving images interact with the seer. The beings under observation sense that they are being monitored. If the vision concerns living human beings, they may suddenly perceive the seer as standing physically near them and address the seer in surprise or puzzlement. This occurs more commonly with spirits while scrying in the astral. Spirits may hold conversations with the seer and attempt to draw him or her into the action of the vision.

If you think about it, these same categories can be applied to ordinary dreams. In some dreams you are merely a watcher; in others you take an active role in events. Many occultists believe that during dreams the astral body separates from the physical body in exactly the same way it does during astral travel. They maintain that there is no essential difference between dreams and astral travel, except that during dreams we are not usually are aware that we are dreaming, and during deliberate astral travel we usually are aware that we are traveling in the astral. However, even this limited distinction is questionable. Lucid dreaming is a widely recognized phenomenon in which the dreamer realizes he or she is asleep during the dream. On the opposite side, it is common for astral travelers to lapse into ordinary sleep.

Entities observed in the mirror have no more power over the scryer than dream entities possess over the dreamer. Yet this power during the dream is considerable. The dreamer escapes the dream by waking up. If such beings could maintain their presence, and thus their power, in consciousness during the day, potentially they could work considerable mischief.

This is the fate of those unfortunate people who are possessed by discarnate Intelligences and continually see spirits, or hear voices, or feel manipulations to their bodies. Imagine, if you can, how difficult it would be to lead a normal life if you constantly heard one or more lower spirits shouting obscenities into your ear in loud, harsh voices, or ordering you to kill yourself or injure someone else. Sleep would become next to impossible. Within a few days you would be in a state of nervous collapse.

For this reason it is useful to be able to clearly and distinctly "wake up" out of the scrying session. The ritual framework of Chapter Seven is designed with this purpose in mind. Once you indraw your magic circle, you explicitly end your communication link with the astral. It is symbolically like hanging up the telephone. By separating your scrying conscious state from your everyday conscious state, you help to insure that spirits will not intrude themselves at awkward times into your awareness either to distract or distress you.

It is tempting to let the visions spill over into ordinary consciousness. Seers who allow this to happen see visions and hear voices at any time of the day or night. So long as the spirits you deal with remain friendly, this poses no threat. If malevolent spirits fix themselves upon you, it is a different story. Communications of an unpleasant nature that can easily be handled for an hour or so every day become intolerable when they intrude constantly at all hours of the day and night.

Whether you look upon spirits as thinking, individual beings with their own purposes and separate existence or you regard them as manifestations of your unconscious mind is a matter of limited interest once you allow the spirits to gain unrestricted access to your awareness.

Mediumship and seership are both a kind of controlled schizophrenia. Seeing visions and hearing voices is not considered a normal activity in our modern society. Even in more primitive cultures it was restricted to shamans and priests, but was regarded as a divine gift rather than a disease. You should bear in mind that when you scry in the mirror you are seeking to alter in a real way the ordinary functioning of your mind, and activate faculties that may be completely dormant.

It has been charged that scrying is nothing more than autohypnosis. I have made an extensive study of hypnosis and see no reason to dispute this assertion. However, it should be understood that hypnosis is one of the most astonishing and mysterious of phenomena. We can manipulate it, we can predict some of its effects, but there is no one on Earth who actually knows what hypnosis is, any more than anyone knows what electricity is in spite of our casual use of it. You read many hypotheses that purport to explain what hypnosis is, but that is all they are, hypotheses, not proof. To call scrying autohypnosis is much the same as calling it a mystery.

9

Astral Travel

Scrying and astral travel are both concerned with the astral world, a region outside ordinary space as we know it, where many of the accepted conventions of time do not apply. For example, it is possible to travel great distances in the astral world in an instant merely by willing it.

When a person enters the astral realm, he or she does not go anywhere physically but passes into an altered state of awareness. The astral world is similar to the dream world, the difference being that in dreams we do not usually know we are dreaming, but in astral travel we usually remain aware that we are traveling, just as we retain our self-awareness when scrying.

In scrying we look at the astral world; in astral travel we enter that world and seem to become a part of it.

By stepping into the astral realm we can gain insight into matters that are beyond the reach of our physical senses, beyond even our consciousness. Circumstances that are gathering at the periphery of our lives and in the future will have great meaning are sometimes manifested astrally, allowing us to gain foreknowledge of important coming events. Emotional dynamics seething below the surface of our minds and driving our actions, forces we do not even suspect to exist, may show themselves in symbolic form in the astral world. Things we could never interact with in the ordinary world—a disease or a childhood trauma, for example—may be confronted, examined, reasoned with, and, if necessary, fought on the plane of the astral. It is possible to talk with a growing field of corn or a mountain, to dance with the sunrise, to direct a swarm of bees or a school of fish because the essences of these things may be translated into conscious forms in the astral capable of communication and a kind of reason.

Spirits, which are at best elusive to common awareness, become tangible in this psychic realm. It is the meeting ground for discarnate, or bodiless, Intelligences in their various recognized forms and human beings. The development of astral vision allows mediums to see ghosts and other such spirits in certain localities. They can be perceived in the astral world superimposed upon the everyday world the way one photographic image may be printed over another.

This, by the way, is why a ghost may be perceptible by sight, sound, touch or odor (rarely taste) to one person, but not to another standing in the same place. The one who sees the ghost is more naturally attuned to astral images and probably has an innate gift for scrying. The same is true of human auras, which clairvoyant individuals see and others do not. Attempts to physically measure auras are futile because auras are an astral manifestation.

Needless to say, for magical work some sensitivity to the astral world is essential. If spirits cannot be perceived, they cannot be communicated with and directed. Also, the effects of magical operations must be monitored so that these operations can be regulated to yield the desired results, and these effects appear first and most strongly in the astral world, and only later manifest physically. Sometimes they do not reveal themselves in the material world at all, or show themselves in widely separated and seemingly unconnected events. To work magic without some degree of astral vision is like trying to sing when you are stone deaf.

Astral travel is the most complete experience of the astral world. It requires a natural talent and considerable practice before it can be done with any degree of ease and confidence. The magic mirror can help to develop the skills of astral travel. In scrying, it acts as a window. In astral travel, it becomes a doorway.

It is best to perform astral travel while seated, either on the floor or on a chair, because there is a natural tendency to fall asleep during the practice if you are lying down. The concentration of the will and the visualization required take energy, and the lower levels of ourselves —our flesh, our feelings and desires—do not wish to make this effort. Consequently, they trick the higher levels—the awareness, the sense of purpose—by producing an intense drowsiness. It is easy to tell that this sleepiness is artificial and not natural because it comes upon the mind almost as soon as the exercise of astral travel is begun. Once it is recognized for what it is, an attempt by one part of ourselves to get out of doing a little work, it can be overcome. But if we lie down during the practice, resistance is harder.

The process of inducing astral travel is similar to that used in autohypnosis. Suggestions are given by the conscious mind in the form of words, images and other mentally created sense impressions to the unconscious level of the mind, which is presumed to be receptive, for the purpose of altering the mental state. Awareness is gradually withdrawn from externally initiated sense impressions and focused upon internally generated images, sounds, feelings and odors. The very act of repeatedly directing the awareness to these internal stimuli induces the transition in an unconscious, automatic manner. It may be likened to cranking the engine of a car with its electric starter motor. At some point the engine fires and begins to run by itself, but first it must be shown the way.

The altered, receptive state occurring during hypnosis is identical to that in the mind of the seer during scrying and astral travel. During hypnosis, the hypnotist controls the astral experience. In astral travel, the experience is controlled jointly by the conscious and unconscious mind of the traveler. In autohypnosis, the experience is regulated by the repeated suggestions given by the conscious mind. Therefore, although the altered state produced by hypnosis and astral travel is essentially the same, the occurrences within that state differ, because in astral travel another controlling influence, the unconscious, acts freely to shape the experience, as it does in dreams.

This unconscious element appears to possess its own awareness. Whether this awareness is single or multiple is more difficult to judge since it acts in ways that suggest both these possibilities, and indeed, perhaps it is one and many simultaneously.

All this is theory and need not worry those who are solely interested in practical astral travel. It is only necessary for you to know that by repeated exercises in which you imagine yourself entering into and moving through an astral place, you will eventually reach a point, if you are persistent and possess an innate talent, when the imagination becomes reality and you actually find yourself passing into another world.

A word must be said about the famous silver cord by which astral travelers are supposed to remain attached to their physical bodies. This was popularized by Sylvan Muldoon in his *Projection of the Astral Body* (Rider, 1929) and reinforced by later writers. There are varying opinions about it. Some say it exists, and its continuance is absolutely necessary for the survival of the physical body. Others say it is a myth. Still others fudge the matter and assert that the cord exists but is made so tenuous by stretching that it cannot be seen.

In my own experiences with astral travel I have never observed the silver cord, even though I have stood looking back at my own reclining body. I believe it to be a visual metaphor of the link between the physical and astral forms, completely real to those who see it, but not inherently necessary for astral travel.

Before attempting astral travel, make sure you can sit in a way that does not require effort or place a strain on your body. It is a virtual necessity to practice sitting until you can sit without noticing any discomfort for at least half an hour; an hour is better. You will need to experiment to find the best position for you. The floor is advisable for beginners. There is some small chance that you may tumble out of your chair when your mind becomes separated from your body, although this rarely happens.

Begin by constructing the ritual circle, then cleanse it and establish the four guardians at the quarters. The mirror should be at eye level or slightly below to avoid neck strain. Make sure there are no reflections visible in the glass. The room must be dark, the only light coming from the candles on either side of the mirror. Anoint your eyelids with the lunar collyrium. It will also help if you wear your charged crystal pendant.

Lunar breathing in the Japanese sitting posture, which is an easier form of the yoga vajrasana pose. I find this position fairly comfortable for up to an hour. It has the advantage of automatically keeping the back straight.

With a short prayer invite the favor and assistance of Selene, goddess of the Moon, since all astral travel falls within her province. It may be useful to invoke the lunar goddess in that form most suited to the astral realm you seek to enter. For example: Diana for all woodlands and natural places on the Earth; Hecate when entering spirit regions; Persephone in communications with shades of the dead.

It is useful to employ a key word to open the mirror, which should be traced lightly upon the surface of the glass with the right index finger and visualized in the form of a thin, glowing line of white light. If you wish to use this method, trace the Enochian word Odo,

which is the verb "open."

Let the Enochian letters fade, and visualize the mirror becoming larger and larger until you lose sight of the edge of the frame. Imagine yourself stepping out of your body and through the plane of the mirror. You may then turn around and look back upon your body to assure yourself that you have left it.

It is best if you preserve a clear sense of yourself within your human form walking into the astral world on two legs because this acts as a stabilizing influence and keeps you from becoming lost in the astral world. Later, when you have some familiarity with astral travel, you may wish to experiment with other forms—that of a bird or a beast, for example. Your astral body is able to assume whatever shape you wish.

This, by the way, is the truth behind werewolf legends. Shamans would project their souls in the form of their totem, the wolf. Many other animals, such as the cat, bear, tiger, eagle, fox, leopard, elk, hawk, and others, were also used in different parts of the world.

When I say you may become lost in the astral world, do not be alarmed. I mean only that you may lose the conscious awareness that you are projecting your astral body and lapse into a state of ordinary dreaming. This holds no danger. You will soon come to yourself sitting within the magic circle. By keeping a firm, continuing awareness of your everyday physical shape, you will find that you are also able to hold more readily to your purpose. This permits more rapid development of the skill of astral projection.

You should have a clear destination in mind when you step into the mirror. This may be an actual physical place, either in the present, past or future. Or it may be an astral world that has no physical counterpart. In either case you are traveling within the astral. Even when you go to a physical place, you are really going to the astral shadow or reflection of that place.

The 22 paths on the Sephirothic Tree of the Kabbalah have proved fruitful for astral travel, as have the astral worlds of the 22 picture cards of the Tarot. In my book *Rune Magic* I describe in detail astral journeys into the worlds of the 24 Germanic runes. The planets, signs of the zodiac, four magical elements, even the levels of heaven and hell as presented in mythology, may all be visited and experienced astrally with little risk.

Similarly, the environments of the gods and goddesses of pagan myth may be entered to engage these potent beings in conversation. It is even possible to enter the Land of the Dead, as the Greek hero Odysseus did in Book X of Homer's *Odyssey*, and talk to those who are no longer living, both near relatives and the great figures of past history. This form of necromancy is not to be entered into lightly, not so much because it is dangerous, but because it can prove disquieting to the unprepared.

When you have finished your astral journey, will yourself once more before the plane of the mirror and look at your seated body on the other side. The astral world you walked through will be replaced by the same featureless uniform darkness that greeted you when you first entered the mirror. Step out through the plane, turn and reseat your astral body within your physical body. Will the mirror to shrink in size and resume its original position and angle upon the table. Open your eyes.

Upon the surface of the glass trace with the nail of your right index finger the Enochian word Allar,

which means "bind up." This will act to seal the plane of the mirror so that no astral inhabitants can cross it against your wishes. It is not necessary to be so careful to bind up the mirror after scrying, where it functions as a window, a thing to be looked through, not passed through. But when the mirror is used as a doorway, it is a prudent practice to place a lock upon it after you are finished using it.

After giving articulate thanks for the successful fulfillment of the ritual purpose, take the time to perform the necessary banishing of unwanted influences and reabsorb the circle. It is never a waste of time to clearly define the boundaries of magic which separate it from the mundane world.

In my view, astral projection invariably involves travel on the astral level. The astral body is never projected in a purely material way into the everyday world, even though this is traditionally held to occur. However, the astral and physical worlds are not distant and distinct places from each other. Both are creations of the mind. They touch. Under certain circumstances which are not clearly understood, they can merge. When this happens, specters are sometimes observed by disinterested individuals, who believe they see these ghosts with their physical eyes. In fact, they are perceiving astral images which have for some reason suddenly become more accessible to ordinary consciousness. This is why not everyone present will see a specter; some are more attuned than others.

When the astral body is perceived, it is seen within the astral world in exactly the same way that ghosts are seen in the astral, not the physical, world. In fact, to the witness there is no obvious difference between the astral traveler and a ghost. Many ghosts may be the astral bodies of those who are traveling, either consciously or unconsciously, in the astral.

Just as the hand of a ghost cannot affect the physical world, neither can the astral body. However, the astral traveler can touch the senses of other people through their minds, causing them to feel a presence. There is no limit to how strong these sensations can be made. Caresses, slaps, even violent blows are perfectly possible. Usually astral bodies are felt as coolness, a faint breeze, a ticklish sensation, or a sting such as might be caused by the prick of a pin or a pinch.

Astral perceptions can prove misleading. Although it seems that some impressions of distant places visited are accurate, others have been wildly in error. Unfortunately, there is no way to tell when a sight seen in the astral corresponds to an event in the physical world. I doubt any astral traveler has developed sufficiently keen judgment to be able to always distinguish a physical event from a purely astral event. Ultimately, the strength of your own conviction must be your guide.

The dangers that confront an astral traveler are

usually the same that face a dreamer. Just as in nightmares you can wake yourself up before you die, so in astral travel you can will yourself instantly back into your physical body when danger threatens. Many writers assert that nothing can keep the astral body from uniting with its physical counterpart if this is strongly desired by the traveler.

Theoretically, there may exist techniques of magic capable of capturing and imprisoning the astral body, just as it is possible to capture a spirit and imprison it within a ring, mirror, or other object. If the astral body were caught and held apart from its physical host, the physical body would subsist in a comatose state until it was reunited with its astral counterpart.

This is a particularly evil subject, and I do not wish to greatly expand upon it here. However, it would not be honest of me to say categorically that such things are impossible and that there is absolutely no danger in astral travel. Dangers of a psychological kind certainly exist. The astral traveler may confront things his conscious mind is not prepared to face, resulting in nervous breakdown or even madness. But such an extreme reaction is highly unusual.

10

Invoking a Familiar

In the fairy tale *Snow White and the Seven Dwarfs* the wicked queen talks to her magic mirror, and the mirror answers her. Although it is not explained in the fairy tale, the voice of the queen's mirror, its awareness and identity, belong to a familiar spirit which the queen has bound within the glass through the use of her occult arts. It is a common practice in magic to place a spirit within an object to lend it power. The resident spirit is thus rendered more accessible because it is kept near at hand and need not be summoned with an elaborate ritual each time it is required.

Familiars, or familiar spirits, are spirits that have a personal relationship with particular human beings. The term "familiar" is most commonly applied to the pet cats, dogs, mice, frogs, or other beasts of medieval witches, but more properly belongs to the spirits dwelling within these animals. Spirits can possess animals just as they can possess human beings. It was convenient for a witch to place her familiar spirit within a domestic beast that could travel with the witch yet remain relatively inconspicuous.

Spirits can also inhabit or be made to inhabit plants, stones and other inanimate things, and even arbitrary positions in space such as a particular spot on the wall. In pagan times many statues were not mere representations of the gods but actual receptacles in which the gods dwelt. By bathing the statues in scented oils or milk, fuming them with appropriate incense, bedecking them with flowers, laying before them offerings of food and drink, praising them with prayers and honoring them with vows and sacrifices, the statues were made inviting places of residence for the gods, each harmonious to the nature of the god within it. For example, a statue of Venus might be entertained with the music of the cithera and the graceful dance of priestesses, while a statue of Mars would hear the clash of swords on shields and watch the athletic dance of warriors.

Magicians are also able to bind spirits into objects against their will. In Shakespeare's *Tempest*, a spirit of the Air named Ariel, familiar of the magician Prospero, had before the arrival of Prospero on the isle where they reside been bound by the witch Sycorax into a tree, as Prospero himself reminds the spirit:

> ...Thou, my slave,
> As thou report'st thyself, wast then her
>   servant:
> And, for thou wast a spirit too delicate
> To act her earthy and abhorr'd commands,
> Refusing her grand hests, she did confine
>   thee,
> By help of her more potent ministers,
> And in her most unmitigable rage,
> Into a cloven pine; within which rift
> Imprison'd, thou didst painfully remain
> A dozen years; within which space she died
> And left thee there, where thou didst vent
>   thy groans
> As fast as a mill-wheels strike...

...Thou best knows't
What torment I did find thee in; thy groans
Did make wolves howl and penetrate the
  breasts
of ever-angry bears: it was a torment
To lay upon the damn'd, which Sycorax
Could not again undo; it was mine art,
When I arriv'd and heard thee, that made
  gape
The pine, and let thee out.
          —*The Tempest*, Act I, Sc. II, ll. 270-93.

I recommend to the reader a close reading of *The Tempest*. Not only is it (in my opinion) Shakespeare's best play, but it contains a wealth of magical and hermetic information.

Although a spirit can be forced to reside in a magical object by symbolically binding its occult sigil—the essence of its being—into the object and compelling the spirit to enter by the authority of more potent Intelligences or gods, there is no point in doing this if you want an obedient, energetic and trustworthy servant. It is far better to make the object an agreeable home for the spirit, who will then willingly enter into it and continue therein with pleasure.

It is also best if you form a good personal rapport with the spirit, who will then act out of love for you, not merely duty. Love fosters love. In order for a spirit to respect and love you, it is necessary for you to genuinely respect and love the spirit, to treat it with consideration and kindness, to show your affection through your words and actions in exactly the same way you would display your affection to a dog, or indeed, to a human companion.

A brief word about the nature of spirits. Spirits

are intelligent, but their intelligence is not the same as human intelligence. They receive impressions very easily, are highly emotional, and change moods from moment to moment. They have no clear understanding of the difference between truth and fiction, and often confuse the two in much the same way a very young child will do. A spirit will tell an untruth not with any intention to mislead but because it senses that this is the answer you wish to hear, and it merely desires to please you. Spirits are easily hurt, and it is as much a moral crime to injure a spirit as it is to torment a living being. Whereas creatures of flesh feel pain most keenly in their bodies, spirits feel pain in their emotions.

The process of inviting a familiar spirit to permanent residence within the magic mirror requires time and effort. It must be done gently. Attracting a familiar is much like trying to get a wild bird to feed out of your hand. You may have to persevere night after night for weeks or months before you get so much as a nibble. However, once you have established the mirror as a meeting place that presents no threat to the spirit but, on the contrary, provides the spirit with pleasure, its presence will become constant and manifest.

It will be necessary for you to repeat your ritual of invocation many times in order for the spirit you wish to attract to become aware that you exist and are inviting its presence. Spirits "see" human beings only when humans create themselves and their works in the astral. When you invoke the spirit into the mirror by focusing your will and imagination upon the glass, the magic circle and other ritual forms, it is as though you and the mirror suddenly popped out of the air in the astral world.

A spirit that feels itself in harmony with the environment you create within the circle will be attracted to it, will learn to recognize you and the name by which you call it, and will come quickly when you summon it in exactly the same way that a wild animal, at first wary and strange, comes to recognize you by the signs you give it, especially by the name you call it, and soon approaches with eagerness.

One of the great secrets of magic, which is not a secret at all but proclaimed everywhere for those with eyes to see it, is that human beings alone possess the power to name things. Beasts cannot name. Neither can angels. But human beings can name both angels and beasts as well as each other. In naming a spirit you gain control over it, because the name you give it—the complete name that defines it, of which the verbal name is only a representation—limits the nature of the spirit. By manipulating the name you can change the environment and perceptions of the spirit. By destroying the name, you can dissolve the spirit into nothingness.

The method of deriving an appropriate name for a spirit is explained fully in Chapter 31 of my book *The New Magus*. For readers who may not be familiar with this work, which contains an abundance of magical techniques and theory, I will briefly repeat the method below.

A lunar spirit should be chosen to dwell within the magic mirror since spirits of the Moon are most in harmony with the work of mirrors. First, consider the general qualities of lunar spirits. What makes a spirit lunar? To arrive at an answer you must know the nature of the Moon itself. Read what you can about the astrological and mythological aspects of the Moon and the lunar goddesses who personify these qualities. Meditate upon the Moon. Actually go outside at night and experience it. Think about the ebb and flow of the tides, the cycles of the human body, growth and decay.

When you think you understand what a lunar spirit is, consider the specific qualities you want and need in the spirit you will invite into your mirror. What uses will the mirror serve? Will it be primarily active or passive? Will it function mainly in a single avenue of life such as business, or healing, or spirit communications?

Visualize the face and body of the ideal lunar spirit to carry out these functions. It is strongly suggested that you confine your imagination to human forms: there is a good reason why angels usually look like men and devils usually appear as monsters. It is also suggested that you picture a spirit of the sex opposite your own, because it is easier to form an emotional bond with a spirit of the opposite sex. Imagine the posture of the spirit, its facial expressions when it talks, its tone of voice and manner of speaking, its way of moving, its clothing. If you have artistic talent, it is useful to draw or paint or sculpt the image of the spirit, but this is not essential, provided you have in your mind the qualities of the spirit and its appearance.

Compress your knowledge of this spirit into a single phrase that embodies as fully as possible its most important aspects. The phrase is a kind of shorthand summary of the spirit. For example, let us suppose that your ideal spirit is a mature woman, not a virgin, tall and slender with long straight black hair that is gathered in a silver clasp behind her neck so that it forms two graceful curves that frame her domed brow and arcing eyebrows. Her eyes are deep brown, her mouth wide, her skin a light olive that makes her small, even teeth shine exceptionally white by contrast when she smiles. She has large strong hands capable of many tasks, which she moves with grace, and a deep knowledge of herbs, stones, beasts, birth, and the growth of things.

You might embody this spirit in the phrase: "Raven-haired mother, skilled in healing and in nurture." The significant words are five. Gather the initial letters of these words, which are: R M S H N. It will usually be necessary to add vowels to make the resulting name pronounceable. When possible, these should be gathered from the words that form the phrase by extending the beginnings of those words. Make your selections in such a way that the final name has seven letters. You may find that you need to rearrange your phrase, reduce it, or even change it entirely to achieve this end.

In the example, the first significant word of the phrase provides the first vowel, and the fourth word the second vowel, for a total of seven letters: Ra M S He N. To this root name is added the suffix El, which in Hebrew signifies God. The name of our hypothetical spirit is Ramshenel, which has nine letters and three syllables, both lunar numbers.

Once the name is perfected, it is necessary to transform it into a visual symbol, called a sigil, that can be easily held in the mind. There are several ways to do this. One of the simplest is described in Chapter 32 of *The New Magus* and involves tracing the pattern of the name upon a spiral wheel of the letters of the alphabet. The letters I and J, plus U and V, are doubled in the same space on the wheel:

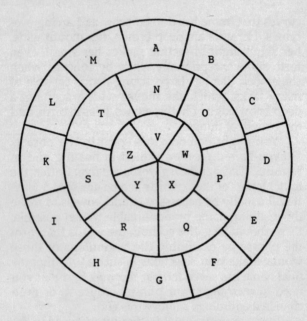

Lay a piece of paper over the wheel and trace a line touching each of the letters in the spirit name, using only the significant letters you initially derived from the phrase. In the case of our example, these letters are R M S H N. They form the sigil illustrated on the following page.

By inscribing this sigil with the right index finger upon the surface of the mirror, by calling the spirit you seek to invoke with the name the sigil represents, and, most importantly, by holding in your mind the nature of the spirit you have conceived and used as the basis for the name and sigil, you can insure that the actual spirit which enters the mirror will correspond closely with the ideal spirit you have imagined. In fact, the actual spirit is formed upon the pattern of the ideal spirit and must correspond to it.

The process of invoking a familiar spirit is straightforward enough, but it requires a considerable devotion of time and effort if it is to be successful. Within the ritual place construct the magic circle, cleanse it and invoke the goddess of the Moon, state your purpose (to call into the mirror the spirit _____ to act as your familiar), then sit before the mirror. Open the mirror with a three-fold clockwise inward spiral.

Trace upon the surface of the glass with your right index finger the sigil of the spirit and allow it to slowly fade away. Call to the spirit by name, at the same time holding in your mind a clear image of the spirit. Ask the spirit to reveal itself. Begin to talk to it as though it were already present, using the same tone and manner you would in confiding your heart to a dear friend. As you do this, scry into the depths of the glass and strive to bring the face of the spirit upward so that it fills the central portion of the mirror.

Always use the most gentle and loving words. Never lie to the spirit or conceal your true purpose. Remember, you are invoking a loving companion who will serve you well if you treat it with respect.

It will help if you create a favorable environment for the spirit. Imagine an astral setting within the mirror that is in harmony with the nature of the spirit. If you are able to travel in the astral, you may want to meet the spirit within this setting. Burn incense of an appropriate kind within the magic circle. If you wish, you can play suitable music to help focus your emotional energy along the line of your will. It is also useful to offer small gifts to the spirit as a sign of your good will and love. These can be offerings of food and drink. The food may be sent to the spirit by burning it until it is completely consumed. The drink may be poured upon the earth.

When you have talked to the spirit for an hour or so, bid it farewell with regret and promise to speak with it again soon. Close the mirror with the circle-cross, give thanks for a successful outcome, and terminate the ritual in the usual way by reversing its steps. When not actually invoking the spirit, it is best to put it completely out of your mind so that it does not intrude upon your daily activities. You will find this quite easy. The ritual will automatically open and seal your mind to the spirit, as it is designed to do.

Once the spirit becomes accustomed to you it will respond quickly when you summon it, even outside the circle. Ritual is not essential in calling the spirit; it merely serves to define the terms upon which you and the spirit will interact. It sets boundaries the spirit will not transgress. When you summon the spirit ritually, you may be fairly confident that it will appear in the expected form and act in the prescribed manner. Spirit communication outside the ritual limits is more apt to hold surprises. Without clear guidelines to follow, the spirit may search for direction and purpose in your storehouse of unconscious impulses. This is what occurs in demonic possession and unstructured mediumship.

The familiar spirit may be used as an aid in scrying. You can order the spirit to bring forth specific images and question the spirit directly on matters that remain obscure. You can send the spirit as a messenger to call other spirits into the mirror for communication, or to induce dreams or visions in living human beings, or to gather information to be conveyed to you in words rather than in images.

I do not wish to mislead the reader. Placing a spirit within the mirror requires fairly advanced magical skills. First, you should gain practice in using the mirror as a scrying instrument. After developing a strong ability to see in the astral and to consciously visualize astral forms, you may begin the lengthy process of calling down a familiar. This entails at least an hour of ritual work each night for several months. You may have success more quickly, but do not count on it. However, once you have acquired the skills to communicate with one spirit, you will find it easier to reach other spirits in a much shorter period of time.

Appendix A

A Simplified Black Mirror

The process described in Chapter Four results in what is probably the most symbolically potent black mirror ever designed. However, it does require carpentry skills and a fair amount of time and labor. Readers who want very much to own and use this magic mirror may feel intimidated by the work of actually making it. Many people with superior mediumistic abilities are poor with their hands.

For those who feel they cannot successfully craft the nine-sided black mirror, or who cannot afford the investment of time it requires, there is a simpler way to make a magic mirror that is both easy and quick. If the mirrors made by this simple method are properly charged, they are nearly as powerful as the nonagon glass.

All you need is a picture frame with a glass front and a cardboard or wooden back. You can buy a new frame designed to hold large photographs, or use an older frame you may find in a flea market or an antique shop or have at home in the attic.

Any frame can be used, but obviously you will wish to select your frame carefully so that it will possess the maximum degree of attractiveness and utility. In magic, utility is in part determined by symbolic correctness. Size is another factor—the frame must not be tiny, yet should be small enough to be easily portable. It must be sturdy to stand up to years of handling and use. A thin, cheap wooden frame held together by staples at the corners is a bad choice because it will fall apart in your hands.

The best material is silver. Old sterling silver mirror frames can sometimes be found, but they are prohibitively expensive. If you happen to own a small, heavy silver frame, you are very fortunate. It will make a wonderful magic mirror.

After sterling silver, silver plate is best, followed by brass. Ebony is the best wood, but rosewood, teak and cherry are also good. Oak should be avoided, because oak is more of a solar than a lunar wood. By the same token, gold or gold-plated frames are solar and will actually inhibit the action of the mirror. Dark woods are better than blond woods.

If the frame is painted, black, white, blue or purple work well, but red, green, yellow and orange are to be avoided. It is not a good idea to paint over a negative color with something more harmonious to the mirror's working because the obstructive color will still exist under the layer of paint and in your mind. If you find the ideal wooden frame in the wrong color, you should use paint stripper and expose the bare wood before you repaint it.

The best shape for the frame is circular, followed in order of preference by oval, hexagonal, octagonal, square and rectangular. Rounded corners are more lunar than sharp corners. A wide frame is more sturdy and attractive than a narrow frame, and will allow the addition of appropriate symbols if desired. Size can range anywhere from six to 24 inches across, but an exposed glass from nine to 12 inches across is the most convenient for regular use.

The glass must be flat and free from scratches and other defects. If you use an antique frame, you may need to replace the glass. Old glass often contains numerous bubbles, occlusions and other defects. These are not too obvious while the glass is clear, but once you have coated it on the inside with black enamel, every tiny scratch or pimple will stand out. Good quality sheet glass works well enough. The frame may not possess a deep enough recess to accommodate plate glass in any case.

New frames can be used just as you buy them from the store. Old frames should be carefully cleaned of all dust and dirt, and polished if they are metal. Remove the glass and clean it on both sides. Then you should perform a simple ritual of cleansing on the old frame and glass to free them of any lingering influences they may have picked up in their years of use. Frames are made to be looked at, and each person who spent time gazing at the picture in the old frame had an emotional reaction to it. If the frame you are using held a family portrait, these emotions may have been very strong and narrow in range. The frame must be purged of these feelings before it will function neutrally.

Collect some water in a small glass vessel from a clear stream, river, or the ocean. Sea water is excellent for cleansing purposes. If fresh water is used, a small amount of natural rock salt should be added to it. A few tiny grains are enough. It is best to draw the water at sunrise, or at least in the early morning before the heat of the day. After you fill the vessel, stand facing east and elevate it so that the morning light shines through it. The water must be perfectly clear without a trace of sediment.

Speak this brief prayer of consecration aloud, or under your breath if others are near:

I dedicate this pure living water in the service of the Light. May it never be defiled.

Visualize the water absorbing the morning light through the transparent sides of the vessel you have used to collect it. When the water seems radiant with light and can hold no more, seal the light in by making the gesture of the circle-cross over the top of the vessel with the index finger of your right hand while holding the vessel in your left hand.

Although the magic mirror is dedicated to the Moon, the office of cleansing belongs to the Sun and the light of the day. That is why the water of cleansing is charged with cool, pure morning light. It is best if the actual rays of the Sun do not shine through the water strongly, since these have an inhibiting action on the power of the Moon. That is why the cleansing water should be drawn in early morning, ideally while the Sun is still in the process of elevating itself above the horizon.

The old frame is cleansed of lingering associations within the context of a simple ritual. Before beginning you should bathe, or at least wash your hands and face so that your own body purity will symbolically contribute to the cleansing process. Put on light clothing and leave your feet bare.

The ritual is best conducted at night before bed when the air is still. It must be done in private. If you do not have a ritual chamber, your bedroom will serve. Place the frame upon the ritual altar, if you use one, or upon a small table such as a bed-

side table. Light a white candle in a brass or si
holder and set it on the altar in the south. Put a
newly bought small bowl of silver, brass or clear
glass on the altar in the north—a plain dessert dish
will serve. Set the sealed crystal vessel of consecrated water on the altar in the west.

Stand to the north of the altar facing south.
Speak the prayer of cleansing and cross your body
as described in Chapter Seven on pages 88-89.
Project a magic circle from your heart center and
cleanse it with the symbols of the four elements.
Establish the guardians of the four quarters outside
the circle and center yourself in the universe. All
these ritual steps, which soon become second
nature, are detailed in Chapter Seven.

After projecting the circle and setting up the
guardians, clearly declare your purpose in conducting the ritual:

> *This ritual is conducted for the purpose of*
> *cleansing the mirror frame and glass upon*
> *the altar.*

Open the vessel of consecrated water and pour
a few ounces into the bowl with your left hand, so
that the stream of water flows from left to right
across your body. Replace the stopper in the vessel
and symbolically seal it again by drawing the circle-cross over its top with your right index finger
while holding the vessel in your left hand.

Setting the vessel aside, dip the index, middle
and ring fingers of your right hand in the bowl to
wet them. These fingers represent the highest trini-
ty of the Sephiroth of the Kabbalah: Kether
(Middle), Chokmah (Ring) and Binah (Index).
Sprinkle the drops of water from your fingers over

.he frame and glass with three deliberate shakes of
your hand. Dip your fingers again and repeat this
threefold gesture. Repeat it a third time so that you
have shaken the water nine times over the frame.

With your three fingers joined, draw in the air
over the frame the Hebrew letter Mem מ so that it
stands in an upright position above the altar about
18 inches tall.

Speak the words:

> *May this pure living water, dedicated to the
> Light, purge this frame and glass, cleansing
> them of all lingering disharmony. So let it
> be.*

Stand facing the south with the altar before
you, your hands pressed together over your heart
in a gesture of prayer. Give thanks to the highest
God, whatever your personal conception of this
deity may be, for the success of the ritual:

> *I thank thee, O Lord, for the fulfillment of
> this ritual for cleansing the mirror frame
> and glass.*

License the four guardians to depart, banish
the perimeter of the circle, then indraw the circle as
described in Chapter Seven. Cross your own body
and declare the end of the ritual. Blow out the candle. Pour the water in the bowl down the sink, saying as you do so: "Return to thy source and remain
undefiled." Dry off the frame and the altar top.
Keep the frame in a secure clean place where it will
not be handled by others or soiled.

I have given this ritual cleansing procedure at
some length because it can be used to cleanse any

object or instrument used in magic. It is possible to do a cleansing more briefly outside the ritual circle with a simple prayer and a sprinkling of pure water, but cleansing is not something that should be done in a negligent way. It produces a clean, white page upon which any desired occult function may be written. Cleansing creates a magical vacuum. A cleansed object is much more strongly dedicated to its new use than one that has not been cleansed because it eagerly absorbs the occult function impressed upon it the way cold metal draws heat from the hand.

Remove the glass from the frame and apply a coating of flat black enamel to the side that has the most scratches, nicks or other defects. To some extent the paint will hide these imperfections. When this has dried, apply a second coat and sprinkle the natural fluid condenser powder over its wet surface.

While the enamel is still wet, pull out three hairs from your head by the roots and press them into the paint so that when the paint dries they will remain bonded into the natural condenser. These hairs represent the physical link between the mirror and its maker and render the mirror a completely personal instrument.

Those who find the ingredients for the natural fluid condenser described in Chapter Three difficult to gather together can make a simpler condenser from equal parts of finely powdered salt, fine silver filings and powdered white eggshell. Natural rock salt is better than table salt, which is full of iodine. Most jewelers will be happy to sell you a small scrap of silver sheet or wire for several times what it is actually worth, or you may use an old piece of sterling silver jewelry. If you use old silver, ritually cleanse it before filing powder from it.

This simple threefold natural condenser will work the same way as the condenser of nine ingredients, but it will not be as potent or as well balanced. There are really no shortcuts in magic—if you do the work, you get the results.

The symbolic fluid condenser is drawn and colored as illustrated in Chapter Three. You will have to make the shape of the actual sheet of paper upon which the nonagon is drawn the same as the shape of the mirror frame, and adjust the size of the figure to fit comfortably behind the glass. The symbols and seals on the symbolic condenser do not need to be drawn perfectly. It is only necessary that you understand what you are doing and what you intend to accomplish while you are drawing them. They must have meaning to you because you are the one who will use the mirror.

Assembling this simple magic mirror is only a matter of sliding the glass into the frame, laying the symbolic fluid condenser over its painted back, and sliding or pinning the cardboard backing into place. In older picture frames the backing may be made of one or more cedar shingles.

Serious thought should be given to replacing any steel nails that secure the backing with nails of brass or silver. Steel is the metal of Mars and a form of iron. Traditionally, sharp steel and cold iron were held to possess the power to hurt and drive away spirits. This is definitely not something you wish to include in a magical instrument for spirit communication, unless you are compelling spirits to serve you against their will. Then the nails could actually act like a ring of threatening sword blades to capture and imprison an unruly spirit, and frighten and torment that spirit into doing your bidding.

It is seldom useful to bully spirits. They react maliciously. More gentle spirits do not need to be forced but will be happy to serve your wishes if your purposes are in harmony with their essential natures. Only if you are involved in very material, chaotic magic intended to hurt others or secure your advantage at the expense of others will it be necessary to resort to lower spirits, which are commonly called demons. These must be compelled by force and threats to serve you.

Not only will higher spirits refuse to perform very gross and evil works, but they are constitutionally incapable of functioning in these labors. Demons can do such work but have a hatred of mankind and only perform such tasks willingly when they believe the magic will backfire against the person who orders it. This, by the way, is the reason dwarfs, who are said to live in the dark bowels of the Earth, are reputed to be treacherous and malicious, plus master craftsmen. They are mythic personifications of the infernal noncorporeal demons and, therefore, embody the demonic qualities.

One advantage this simplified black mirror possesses over the nine-sided glass is the ease with which the sigil of a particular spirit can be slipped into the frame beneath the cardboard or wooden backing. This can be a great aid in drawing a spirit with the qualities you require into the mirror and keeping it there. If you later discover that you need a spirit with different qualities, the spirit sigil can be taken out and ritually destroyed to release the resident spirit from the mirror, with another different sigil representing the qualities of the second spirit placed beneath the backing of the frame.

It is even possible to retain a set of sigils to be interchanged at will in answer to present need so that no single spirit is resident in the mirror on a continuing basis, but a number of familiar spirits with different special functions are always within easy call. Sets of spirit sigils can be made for the four elements, the seven traditional planets, or the 12 signs of the zodiac. They can also be selected from the hierarchy of Enochian spirits or from the angels of the Kabbalah.

Appendix B

Table of Hebrew Letters

In the Kabbalah all power and meaning rests in the 22 letters of the Hebrew alphabet, which convey the sacred words of God to mankind via the holy books. There is magic not only in the sounds of the letters but in their very shapes, and even in the white spaces on the page that surround and are defined by them.

Since the shape of the letters is so important, an effort should be made to copy them accurately onto the symbolic fluid condenser. The easiest way for those unfamiliar with Hebrew is to draw the outline of each letter with a sharp pencil, then trace and fill them in with black ink. Take care to distinguish the subtle differences between similar letters such as Gimel and Nun, Beth and Kaph, He and Cheth, Daleth and Resh, and Ayin and Tzaddi.

The Hebrew alphabet has no vowels. Vowel sounds are indicated by small marks, called points, near the letters. However, in magic unpointed Hebrew is used almost exclusively for seals and amulets.

Five of the letters—Kaph, Mem, Nun, Pe and Tzaddi—have an alternate form called a "final" form because they are used only when these letters occur at the end of words. Since no final forms appear on the symbolic fluid condenser, I have not represented them in the table.

Table of Hebrew Letters

Letters	Sound	Name
א	A	Aleph
ב	B, V	Beth
ג	G, Gh	Gimel
ד	D, Dh	Daleth
ה	H	He
ו	O, U, V	Vau
ז	Z	Zayin
ח	Ch	Cheth
ט	T	Teth
י	I, Y	Yod
כ	K, Kh	Kaph

Table of Hebrew Letters

Letters	Sound	Name
ל	L	Lamed
מ	M	Mem
נ	N	Nun
ס	S	Samekh
ע	Aa, Ngh	Ayin
פ	P, Ph	Pe
צ	Tz	Tzaddi
ק	Q, K	Qoph
ר	R	Resh
ש	S, Sh	Shin
ת	T, Th	Tau

Appendix C

Table of Enochian Letters

These are the forms of the letters as they were drawn by Edward Kelly on May 6, 1583, and preserved in the British Museum Library manuscript Sloane 3188, folio 104. When Kelly was first shown the letters by the spirits, he found that he could not copy them accurately. The spirits caused the Enochian letters to appear on the paper before him in a light yellow color. Kelly then traced the outlines of the letters in black ink with his pen, and the yellow originals faded away, leaving only the black, which he filled in. The letters are drawn on the manuscript page from right to left in two rows. The top row contains 11 letters and ends with Ur, the bottom row, the remaining ten.

Although simplified and stylized versions of the Enochian alphabet have been used by modern occultists, the only truly correct forms of the letters are those received by Kelly directly from the spirits and traced by him. This tracing also reveals the correct angle of the letters—sometimes in modern occult works letters appear tilted to the left or right.

Table of Enochian Letters

Letter	Sound	Name
V	B	Pa
B	C, K	Veh
b	G, J	Ged
X	D	Gal
X	F	Or
X	A	Un
7	E	Graph
E	M	Tal
Z	I, Y	Gon
M	H	Na
L	L	Ur

Table of Enochian Letters

Letter	Sound	Name
Ω	P	Mals
Ᵽ	Q	Ger
Ƽ	N	Drux
Γ	X	Pal
Ɔ	O	Med
Ɛ	R	Don
Ꝗ	Z	Ceph
Ꝋ	U, V	Van
٦	S	Fam
◢	T	Gisg

STAY IN TOUCH

On the following pages you will find listed, with their current prices, some of the books and tapes now available on related subjects. Your book dealer stocks most of these, and will stock new titles in the Llewellyn series as they become available. We urge your patronage.

To obtain a FREE COPY of our latest full CATALOG of New Age books, tapes, videos, crystals, products and services, just write to the address below. In each 80 page catalog sent out bimonthly, you will find articles, reviews, the latest information on New Age topics, a listing of news and events, and much more. It is an exciting and informative way to stay in touch with the New Age and the world. The first copy will be sent free of charge and you will continue receiving copies as long as you are an active customer. You may also subscribe to *The Llewellyn New Times* by sending a $2.00 donation ($7.00 for Canada & Mexico, and $20.00 for overseas). Order your copy of *The Llewellyn New Times* today!

The Llewellyn New Times
P.O. Box 64383-Dept. 831, St. Paul, MN 55164

TO ORDER BOOKS AND PRODUCTS
ON THE FOLLOWING PAGES:

If your book dealer does not carry the titles and products listed on the following pages, you may order them directly from Llewellyn. Just write us a letter. Please add $2 for postage and handling for orders of $10 and under. Orders over $10 require $3.50 postage and handling. (USA and in US funds). UPS Delivery: We ship UPS whenever possible. Delivery guaranteed. Provide your street address as UPS does not deliver to P.O. Boxes; UPS to Canada requires a $50 minimum order. Allow 4-6 weeks for delivery. Orders outside the USA and Canada: Airmail—add $5 per book; add $3 for each non-book item (tapes, etc.); add $1 per item for surface mail.

Send orders to:

LLEWELLYN PUBLICATIONS
P.O. Box 64383-831
St. Paul, MN 55164-0383, U.S.A.

HOW TO DREAM YOUR LUCKY LOTTO NUMBERS
By Raoul Maltagliati

Lotteries and sweepstakes are becoming increasingly popular, as people from many U.S. states wait hopefully for their chance at riches. Now Llewellyn introduces a book that no wishful lotto contestant could pass up.

How to dream your lucky lotto numbers is one of three exciting, mass-market how-to books coming this spring. Here Raoul Maltagliati tells.

- **How this system works**
- **How to discover the numeric value of various dream subjects**
- **How to interpret dreams**
- **And much more**

A comprehensive dream dictionary gives the meanings of various dreams, while letting the reader quickly find the numbers associated with a given dream.

The author also presents the underlying theory of dream analysis, information on the lotto, and an interview with an actual dream analyst who advises people on their lotto numbers.

0-87542-483-X, mass market, illus. $3.95

HOW TO MAKE AN EASY CHARM TO ATTRACT LOVE INTO YOUR LIFE
by Tara Buckland

Everyone wants a happy love life. In today's world, singles organizations thrive on this fact, as divorce and increased personal independence create more love-hungry people than ever. In this book, Buckland presents:

- **An intorudction to magick**
- **A quiz for the person seeking love**
- **Egyptian love spells**
- **Techniques for building an Egyptian love amulet**

Buckland, an authority on Egyptian magick, explains the importance of magick in the ancient land, how the relatively unattractive Cleopatra used it to attract many lovers, and how the Egyptians' ancient knowledge is especially pertinent today.

0-87542-087-7, mass market, illus. $3.95

THE LLEWELLYN PRACTICAL GUIDE TO ASTRAL PROJECTION.
by Denning and Phillips
Is there life-after-death? Are we forever shackled by time & space? The ability to go forth by means of the Astral Body, or Body of Light, gives the personal assurance of consciousness (and life) beyond the limitations of the physical body. No other answer to these ageless questions is as meaningful as experienced reality.

The reader is led through the essential stages for the inner growth and development that will culminate in fully conscious projection and return. Not only are the requisite practices set forth in step-by-step procedures, augmented with photographs and puts-you-in-the-picture" visualization aids, but the vital reasons for undertaking them are clearly explained. Beyond this, the great benefits from the various practices themselves are demonstrated in renewed physical and emotional health, mental discipline, spiritual attainment, and the development of extra faculties".

0-87542-181-4, 272 pgs., 5¼ x 8, illus., softcover   **$7.95**

SIMPLIFIED MAGIC
by Ted Andrews
A person does not need to become a dedicated Qabalist in order to acquire benefits from the Qabala. *Simplified Magic* offers a simple understanding of what the Qabala is and how it operates. It provides practical methods and techniques so that the energies and forces within the system and within ourselves can be experienced in a manner that enhances growth and releases our greater potential.

The Qabala is more than just some theory for ceremonial magicians. It is a system for personal attainment and magic that anyone can learn and put to use in his or her life. The secret is that the main glyph of the Qabala, the Tree of Life, is *within* you. The Tree of Life is a map to the levels of consciousness, power and magic that are within. By learning the Qabala you will be able to tap into these levels and bring peace, healing, power, love, light and magic into your life.
0-87542-015-X, 210 pgs., illus., softcover   **$3.95**

ENOCHIAN MAGIC—A Practical Manual
by Gerald J. Schueler

The powerful system of magic introduced in the sixteenth century by Dr. John Dee, Astrologer Royal to Queen Elizabeth I, and as practiced by in the sixteenth century by Dr. John Dee, Astrologer Royal to Queen Elizabeth I, and as practiced by Aleister Crowley and the Hermetic Order of the Golden Dawn, is here presented for the first time in a complete, step-by-step form. *There has never before been a book that has made Enochian Magic this easy!*

In this book you are led carefully along the path from "A brief history of the Enochian Magical System," through "How to Speak Enochian," "How to Invoke," "The Calls," "Egyptian Deities" and "Chief Hazards" to "How to visit the Aethyrs in Spirit Vision (Astral Projection)." Not a step is missed; not a necessary instruction forgotten.

0-87542-710-3, 270 pgs., 5¼ x 8, illus., softcover $12.95

A KABBALAH FOR THE MODERN WORLD
by Migene Gonzalez-Wippler

The Kabbalah is the basic form of Western mysticism, and this is an excellent manual of traditional Kabbalistic Magick! It contains one of the best introductions to the Kabbalah ever written.

If you have ever been intimidated by the Kabbalah in the past, and never studied its beauty, *this is the book for you*. It clearly and plainly explains the complexities of the Kabbalah. This is an ideal book for newcomers to the study of Kabbalah or mysticism and spirituality in general.

This book covers a variety of Kabbalistic topics including: Creation, the nature of God, the soul and soul mates, the astral and other planes, the four worlds, the history of the Kabbalah, Bible interpretation and more.

A Kabbalah for the Modern World is written so clearly that it makes complex kabbalistic ideas easy to understand. This book needs to be in the library of every occultist, Pagan, Kabbalist, mystic and person involved in the New Age.

0-87542-294-2, 240 pages, 5¼ x 8, illus. $9.95

THE NEW MAGUS
by Donald Tyson
The New Magus is a practical framework on which a student can base his or her personal system of magic.

This book is filled with practical, usable magical techniques and rituals which anyone from any magical tradition can use. It includes instructions on how to design and perform rituals, create and use sigils, do invocations and evocations, do spiritual healings, learn rune magic, use god-forms, create telesmatic images, discover your personal guardian, create and use magical tools and much more. You will learn how *YOU* can be a *New Magus!*

The New Age is based on ancient concepts that have been put into terms, or *metaphors*, that are appropriate to life in our world today. That makes *The New Magus* the book on magic for today.

If you have found that magic seems illogical, overcomplicated and not appropriate to your lifestyle, *The New Magus* is the book for you. It will change your ideas of magic forever!

0-87542-825-8, 6 x 9, illus., softcover.   **$12.95**

RUNE MAGIC
by Donald Tyson
Drawing upon historical records, poetic fragments, and the informed study of scholars, *Rune Magic* resurrects the ancient techniques of this tactile form of magic, and integrates those methods with modern occultism, so that anyone can use the runes in a personal magical system. For the first time, every known and conjectured meaning of all 33 known runes, including the 24 runes known as *futhark*, is available in one volume. In addition, *Rune Magic* covers the use of runes in divination, astral traveling, skrying, and on amulets and talismans. A complete rune ritual is also provided, and 24 rune words are outlined. Gods and Goddesses of the runes are discussed, with illustrations from the National Museum of Sweden.

0-87542-826-6, 210 pgs., 6 x 9, illus., softcover   **$9.95**

CHARMS, SPELLS AND FORMULAS
by Ray Malbrough

In this book, Ray Malbrough reveals to you the secrets of Hoodoo magick. By using the simple materials available in Nature, you can bring about the necessary changes to greatly benefit your life and that of your friends. You are given detailed instructions for making and using the *gris-gris* (charm) bags only casually or mysteriously mentioned by other writers. Malbrough not only shows how to make gris-gris bags for health, money, luck, love and protection from evil and harm, etc., but he also explains how these charms work.

He also takes you into the world of *doll magick;* using dolls in rituals to gain love, success, or prosperity. Complete instructions are given for making the dolls and setting up the ritual.

Hoodoo magick can be as enjoyable as it is practical, and in this fascinating book you can learn how to be a *practitioner*, working your spells and charms for yourself or for others. Learn the methods which have been used successfully by Hoodoo practitioners for nearly 200 years, along with many practical tips for dealing with your clients.

0-87542-501-1, 192 pgs., 5¼ x 8, illus., softcover $6.95

THE COMPLETE BOOK OF INCENSE, OILS AND BREWS
by Scott Cunningham

Scott Cunningham, world-famous expert on magical herbalism, first published *The Magic of Incense, Oils and Brews* in 1986. *The Complete Book of Incense, Oils and Brews* is a revised and expanded version of that book. Scott took readers' suggestions from the first edition and added more than 100 new formulas. Every page has been clarified and rewritten, and new chapters have been added.

There is no special, costly equipment to buy, and ingredients are usually easy to find. The book includes detailed information on a wide variety of herbs, sources for purchasing ingredients, substitutions for hard-to-find herbs, a glossary, and a chapter on creating your own magical recipes.

0-87542-128-8, 288 pgs., 5¼ x 8, illus., softcover $12.95